Elsie Milla

WITHIN THE HEART

OF GOD, I AM

DARE TO SEE YOUR OWN BEAUTY

Lucero Tello, MorningStar

 FriesenPress

Suite 300 - 990 Fort St
Victoria, BC, V8V 3K2
Canada

www.friesenpress.com

Copyright © 2020 by Lucero Tello, MorningStar
First Edition — 2020

Lucero Tello is not a doctor, psychologist or medical counseling. The suggestions included in this book do not intend to dispense medical advice or recommend any technique as replacement for any physician treatment. In the event you use any of the information in this book for yourself, which is your constitutional right, the author and the publisher assume no responsibility for your actions.

All rights reserved.

No part of this publication may be reproduced in any form, or by any means, electronic or mechanical, including photocopying, recording, or any information browsing, storage, or retrieval system, without permission in writing from FriesenPress.

ISBN
978-1-5255-6286-0 (Hardcover)
978-1-5255-6287-7 (Paperback)
978-1-5255-6288-4 (eBook)

1. RELIGION, MYSTICISM

Distributed to the trade by The Ingram Book Company

TABLE OF CONTENTS

INTRODUCTION	1
CHAPTER I	
LIFE-CHANGING EXPERIENCES	7
The Voice of God	8
Fighting My Unworthiness	8
God Is Smiling!	10
Smile-Pillows Experience	10
The Hands of God in a Photograph	12
"Write the Memories of Your Life"	
I Am That I Am	13
Running Away from My Purpose?	13
CHAPTER II	
MYSTICAL EXPERIENCES AND PILGRIMAGES	15
The First Photograph that Opened the Door to My Awakening	15
A Blue Bird Came to Me	22
The Animal Kingdom Helped a Missing Boy in North Carolina	23
Alaska Whales, A Show of Joy	24
A Golden Bird Shape in the Sky	25
Angels Holding the Plane	25
A Little Lost Soul in My Home	26
A Bird's Visitor	27
Colorful Clouds—Love and Support from the Sky	27
A Bird's Convention by My Deck	28
A Rattle Snake	28
Chemtrails in Sedona and in Florida	28
A Bird's Love Story	29
Divine Love	29
Michael Jackson	30
Soul Retrieval at the Hualapai Indian Reservation	30

Reflection ... 32
PILGRIMAGES ... 32
The John of God Experience—Brazil ... 32
The House of John of God- Brazil ... 33
Meditation after the Event ... 35
Camino De Santiago Pilgrimage - Spain ... 36
The Mount of Forgiveness ... 36
Archangel Michael's Golden Boots ... 37
Himalayan Trekking ... 38
Ancient Attraction ... 38
The Experience ... 39
A Remarkable Encounter—The Divine Feminine ... 40
Divine Lesson ... 41
Going Back to Our Starting Point ... 42
Recovering Codes in the Himalayas ... 44
Nepal Overview ... 44
The Kopan Monastery Visit in Kathmandu, Nepal ... 44
France Pilgrimage ... 45
"Nothing That Oppresses You Can Be Further from the Truth" ... 45

CHAPTER III
HEALING ABILITIES–A GIFT ... **49**
My First Clients—Baby Chicken ... 49
The Empath in Me ... 49
First Healing Modalities I Practiced ... 51
Star Healing Intergalactic Energy and Divine Mother Healings ... 51
Receiving Downloads to Practice
My Own Healing Modality ... 51
Light Coming from My Hands—I Am an Electric Conduit of Healing ... 51
A Neighbor Came for Lunch and was Healed ... 52
Healing a Lady at Walmart (Murphy, NC) ... 53
An Interesting Approach I Discerned When Assisting Two People ... 54
Heal the Root of the Situation to Heal the Physical Pain ... 54
Lesson I Learned ... 55
My Favorite Technique ... 55
Some Testimonials ... 56

CHAPTER IV
MY LIBERATION — 57

The Deepest Part of The River — 57
Growing Up in Colombia — 58
Healing Archetypal Patterns Together — 59
Becoming Aware of Her Dark Side — 59
Opening My Heart to Compassion — 60
Reflection — 61
Another Truth Came Afloat During A Psychic Healing Session-
Child Molestation — 62
First Marriage Experience — 63
An Event that Opened the Door to Forgiveness — 65
Second Husband Trapped in the Astral Level — 65
Third Husband, Another Nightmare — 67
I Became an Object — 68
My Awakening — 68
Separation Process—Leaving the House — 68
His Harassment in Sedona, Arizona — 70
I Filled My Third Ex-husband's Heart with Divine Light — 71
A Celestial Solution — 71
Another Case with Similar Energy — 71
The Last One — 73
The Final Piece of the Puzzle — 74
God's Promise — 77
More Clearing in the Back of My Heart — 77
The Last Resource I Used - It Worked — 78
Healing Psychic Attacks with the Energy of Love — 78
More Tests of Initiation—A Snake — 78
The Power of Forgiveness — 79

CHAPTER V
YOUR LIBERATION — 83

All Your Wishes Are Attainable — 84
General Recommendations — 87
Let's Get Started! — 87

Practices & Meditations	88
Exercise 1. Grounding	88
Exercise 2. The Power of Gratitude	88
Exercise 3. Delete Button to Release Unwanted Attachments	89
Exercise 4. Forgiveness Therapy	90
First Day:	90
Second Day:	91
Step Two of Second Day:	91
Exercise 5. Meditations	92
Exercise 6. Add Visualizations to Your Meditation Practice	93
Exercise 7. Self-Love Exercise	93
Exercise 8. Relationships	95
Exercise 9. The Importance of Journaling	96
Exercise 10. Work Out	97
Exercise 11. The Power of Fasting—Detoxifying the System	97
More Loving Suggestions	97
Massaging the Brain to Release Stress	97
Retrain Your Thoughts with the Power of the Heart to Change Your Reality	97
The Heart Is a Generating Love Machine	98
Before Leaving the House	99
At a Public Place	99
Dissolving a Traffic Jam with Love!	99
In Oneness with Gaia	99
Bringing Love to Gaia and Her Inhabitants	100
Beating Cold Temperatures	100
Clearing Negativity in My Computer—Mind Control	101
Getting Bugs out of the House—Insects' Consciousness	101
Clearing Plants	102
Vacuum Exercise to Keep a Translucid Energy Field	102
The Dangers of Sugar	103
View on Politics—Young Creators	103

CHAPTER VI
CHRIST CONSCIOUSNESS   105

A Photo, a Message, and a Meditation	105
Using the Light of The Christ	106
Photograph and a Short Dialogue with Him	107
Devotion	108
A Fourth-Pointed Star in A Circle	110
Mahavatar Babaji	110
His Second Message Said: "I Live in Your Heart."	111
"Every Beating of Your Heart Is a Remembrance of My Soul"	111
Cobra Breath	112
The Story of Sanat Kumara—A Planetary Logos	112
Spiral of Light from Sanat Kumara's Book	113
Oneness Vision	113
In Honor of Archangel Michael	114
My Story with Archangel Michael	114
"Dear and Glorious Physician"	116

CHAPTER VII
DIVINE MOTHER   117

Who Is Divine Mother?	117
My Connection with Divine Mother	118
Divine Mother Tools	118
A Friend's Parents Went into the Light Many Years after Passing	119
Healing Many Entities or Lost Souls at Once	120
Guiding Lost Souls to Find Their Way Home Is a Privilege	121
I Have Been a Lost Soul, Too!	121
Reflection	122
Maria Magdalene's Message to Humanity through Judith K. Moore	122
A Vision of The Crucifixion	125
Damage from the Catholic Church Teachings	126
Mother Mary	126
The Queen of Heaven	126
"I Want the World to See My Tears"	128
God's Calling Us Back Home	130

Stairway to Heaven — 131
Heaven on Earth — 132

CHAPTER VIII
MY CREATIONS - GOD AND ME — 135
The Story Around Them — 135
I Am Healthy—I Am Beautiful — 136
I Love Myself — 137
The Frequency of Gratitude — 138
The Energy Of Devotion — 139
Inner Peace — 140
A Thought I Wrote on 5/28/17 — 140
I Am Enough — 141
Love and Respect for Our Children — 141
Scientific Proof That God Lives in Our Hearts — 143

CHAPTER IX
GALACTIC COMMAND-CONFEDERATION — 145
Galactic—Photographs — 145
Who Are the Galactics? — 146
The Arcturians — 147
An Unusual Experience—A Mermaid — 148
Alcazar and the Stargate — 148
Learnings from The Stargate Experience — 149
A Photograph of Sedona, Arizona — 150
The Hathors — 151

ACKNOWLEDGMENTS — 153

ABOUT THE AUTHOR — 155

**To the Smiling
God the Father
God the Mother
God the Child**

I wrote this book with an open heart, a heart full of gratitude to our Infinite Source of Love. May my writing be nothing but a humble tribute to the Divine Presence within.

Thank you for holding my hand all the way, for making me feel important and charged with a mission, for rescuing me when I was lost, for reminding me how to open my heart to unconditional love and Oneness for All that Is.

Please grant me the honor to be a conduit of your love, of your humbleness, of your peace, of your healing.

I Adore You!

Forever Thankful

To Mother Mary's constant assistance as a representative of the Sacred Feminine Force, the Angelic Realm, the Galactic Command, the Divine Masters.

To my Earthly Angels, Felipe and Alejandra, for their unconditional support. To my heavenly granddaughter, Salma, and to my earthly family, teachers and friends.

INTRODUCTION

Beloved Brother-Sister,
Consider this manuscript a resource of divine messages and divine photographs. Even if the content does not appeal to you, come back and recreate your soul with the power they contain.

"I am the way the truth and the life.
I am perfection everywhere.
I am the light. I am the truth. I am God.
I am Mother Father God.
Keep writing; you will get to a point where you will find the truth."
Me: What truth?
"The Truth of what you are. The truth of who you are."
Me: Is that relevant for my mission on Earth?
I only heard:
"I am here with you."

Dear reader,
I have written this book with the genuine intention to encourage you to open your heart to yourself. Yes, to yourself! From that perspective, you will uncover the unparalleled potential that resides in there, empowering your soul enough to unlock your sacred gifts.
I would like to invite you to fly with me into the world of miracles through my genuine, pure stories. When I had the audacity to break the attachments that were preventing me from reaching my desired freedom and finally jumping into the infinite Source of Love, God-Goddess, my life changed dramatically.
The journey has not been easy. It took me a great deal of tears and conscious inner healing to be able to share the whole package, the good and not-so-good stories. The challenge was to accept them with an open heart. Through the ordeal, I discovered I was ashamed of allowing others to abuse me. I tried to hide it with silence. It was a psychological battle.

My soul had been wandering. Distraught by the betrayals and lies of those who had sworn to love me, I was looking outside for what I could have easily found within. Once I became aware of my inner power, I found solace my soul craved.

It took me a few years to beat my insecurities, trust my divine intuition, and begin this endeavor. As I did, a rush of excitement began surging, propelling me to persist.

At this moment, I am singing in joy, getting goosebumps all over as a validation that my prayers have been heard and my writing shall serve its purpose; my story will act as a catalyst and inspire you to share yours as well. Each person has a story to tell. I am waiting for yours!

Now, let me present to you what is inside this book.

First of all, a poignant message from Mother/Father God just for you.

Chapter I: Events that Changed My Life Forever-The Voice of God/God's Hands in a photograph.

In this chapter appears the very first photograph I received showing the Galactic Appearance; this event opened the door to my awakening. Also, detailed information about how and when I began hearing the Voice of God. The trail of tears I went through to break many negative beliefs that were stopping me from seeing the truth of who I am. The hands of God in an amazing photograph. Did you know that God smiles? She/He communicates with us through simple details that we don't even realize! Read the whole story.

Chapter II. Personal Mystical Experiences
Even though some stories may seem hard to believe, they are authentic. Details about different pilgrimages are included.

Chapter III. My Healing Abilities—Light Coming from My Hands
The human body carries electricity. I am a positively charged battery, making it easier for me to provide healings. I am ready and humble to channel God's healing. It includes a few commentaries from clients.

Chapter IV. My Ordeals—My Liberation
Provides a short description of my life and includes events that played an important role in my metamorphosis. I describe the changes I've made

and how I've developed, as well as the Divine Beings that assisted me. I also describe how I detached myself from my past to embrace a new me.

Chapter V. Unleashing Your Chains
It is time to unlock the power of our hearts. I have listed the steps to assist you in unlocking your potential to reach abundance and joy. Here are meditations, practices, and exercises that will support you achieving in this endeavor.

Chapter VI. Second Coming of Jesus Christ
Two impressive photographs holding important meanings.

The amazing and mysterious figure called Jesus Christ awaits you with His powerful messages filled with incommensurable and eternal love. He has been by our side the whole time, and He appears more powerful and stunning than ever through the photographs exhibited here. I asked about the meaning of the one showing an encircled four-pointed hologram. It intrigued me enormously. I heard: "The Second Coming of Christ." Another one displays His mighty light, which can assist in raising our Christ Consciousness. A third one shows the sign of the cross.

In addition, I share Archangel Michael's revelation to me. Am I an aspect of Saint Luke? See his answer inside. More information about the Master of Masters: The Eternal Babaji and "The Cobra Breath," his gift to humanity. I also give recognition to a wonderful and humble being named Sanat Kumara, the Planetary Logos.

Chapter VII. Divine Feminine—Divine Mother—Mother Mary
The Infinite Wisdom and Love of Divine Mother may touch you so deeply that you may get inspired to find out more about Her. How can it be possible that we also have a Mother God and were not aware of that? Many questions are simultaneously simple and complex. She has been waiting to have an intimate, personal relationship with you. Mother Mary, the Queen of Angels, said to me: "I want the world to see my tears." Read the whole story about her message for humanity. Her light and compassion will assist your heart, as will some of my first paranormal experiences and insight on how to heal earthbound spirits with love.

Chapter VIII. Lucero's Creations

Master Wyamus came forth and advised me to draw. My first reaction was one of disbelief. Later, divinely inspired, I began doing it. Each one has its respective meaning.

Chapter IX. The Galactic Command—My Origin

The wondrous Galactic Federation/Confederation of Light appeared in my photographs in 2014. Their message is included. They are displayed not just in this chapter but throughout the book.

I just discovered my deep connection with The Hathors.

My Perspective of God:

I would like to add that, from my perspective, God encompasses both the Feminine and Masculine aspects. You may find different names for God throughout the book. I use them interchangeably, such as Mother/Father God, She or He, Infinite Source of Love, or the Nameless One.

Gracias, divine reader, for taking the time to be with me.

Blessings,
MorningStar

A Poignant Message from Mother-Father God Just for You

I am here with you.
I give you shelter.
I give you light.
I wrap you up constantly.
My Love is incommensurable, unlimited.
I protect you. I hold you in my arms.
I love you. I guide you.
I enlighten you.
Do not step out.
Do not let the illusion of the world disconcert you.
You are perfect!
You are my child.
If you are cold, I will warm you up.
If you are hungry, I will feed you.
If you are in doubt, I will calm you.
You are my most beautiful creation.
I love you!

CHAPTER I
LIFE-CHANGING EXPERIENCES

Divine Messages

It is a great honor to share with you how I began to receive divine messages, along with the emotions that catapulted my spiritual awakening.

It all started when my second husband, whom I had divorced, passed away. His soul came to me for assistance. This event made me search for deep answers about reincarnation, karma, lost souls and, in general, whatever goes beyond human comprehension. I began meditating.

Years later, I found Divine Mother classes online. Through them, my intuition and life perspective opened up considerably. I extended my meditations into the wee hours of the morning. And then something outrageous happened: A magnificent presence who called Himself "Mother-Father God" communicated with me, as did Master Sananda, Jesus the Christ, Mother Mary, Mahavatar Babaji, Saint Peter, Maria Magdalene, and other divine beings. One time, a message began with: "You may call me The Nameless One." I received several messages, which I wrote in the dark with my eyes closed. They are included in this volume for you to receive with an open heart.

"I am the Nameless One.
I come in the name of God.
I come in the name of truth.
I am here to teach you that there is nothing more
Powerful than the word of God."

The Voice of God

One afternoon in 2015, while attending one of Divine Mother's classes, my right hand began to shake, as had been happening lately. When I asked for its meaning, I heard the following:

"I AM MOTHER/FATHER GOD.
I want you to write my messages.
When are you going to do that?
I am waiting for you.
I want you to write a book."

At the end, I heard: "*Conversations with God.*" I was speechless, and my entire body trembled. As I broke into tears, I vividly recalled that I had actually bought the book *Conversations with God,* by Neale Donald Walsh earlier, but had reluctantly kept it on my bookshelf. After calming myself down, I began reading it. This great book assisted me in understanding God's wisdom and finding the courage to publicly acknowledge that Mother/Father God had been communicating with me and that celestial lights from other galaxies had appeared in my photographs. Nevertheless, an internal battle started around the idea of writing a book. A book? Who was I, anyway? How can God talk to someone like me? He wants to give me His messages? All my doubts, insecurities and sense of unworthiness came out to make fun of me and diminish the beauty of the event. The insecurity took over, and I did not write anything for a while.

Fighting My Unworthiness

Later, I heard the voice again, this time telling me to write about myself. My first reaction was: What? About my life? Do you want me to write about my life? About those events that caused so much pain? The only thing I heard was a Yes. I unenthusiastically began writing from my past. Little did I know that by translating my pain into words, I was healing my wounds. The more I wrote, the more I healed.

One-time, Divine Mother came to me with the following wisdom: "*Your story does not belong to you,*" she said. "*It is the story of the world; it is the story of humanity. Others will identify with it.*"

I said: "*If my writing serves as an inspiration to someone, I will write with great love in my heart.*"

Here are some thoughts from my journal:

"*God talked to me! What? To me? And He wants me to write a book! Impossible! How can that be? As if the idea of receiving photographs from other galaxies was not enough to get me out of my comfort zone. This must have been a mistake. Let's ignore it and keep living what seems like a normal life like any other human being.*"

Later on, I wrote: "*Let's suppose that it's true. What am I going to write about? How can I begin such a journey? Who can I tell that God wants me to write a book?*" I kept it quiet, just debating the same questions over and over again, day and night. What a nightmare! How can the voice and command of God become a nightmare? I am so ungrateful." All these thoughts and emotions tortured me for four years. However, I kept journaling my daily life.

At times, I used to sit looking at the computer, as if I was hoping to receive instructions from it! I wondered what my Nameless One (that is the name He/She said I could call Him) wants me to write. I have been writing my thoughts, complaints, dreams, and how I feel toward Him, but I do not know what to include. I am crying again! This is driving me nuts!"

Another page says: "Mother-Father God, even though I wish to write with all my heart, I'm still wondering what I am supposed to write about. Should I start by talking about the adoration I profess toward you, how grateful I am to be able to hear your voice and acknowledge that you are interested in my writing? What writing? I have not written anything important so far!"

I would say that my biggest trouble was to admit that God wanted me to write a book. I am thrilled, but at the same time so stressed out! A war broke out (or erupted) inside me. I haven't had peace since then. Many questions came into my small mind. "Why has He chosen me? Is this true? How am I going to write a book when my primary language is not even English?" Many doubts were trying to stop me from even accepting the idea. It took me four years to sit and organize my writings until this project was completed in 2019.

God Is Smiling!

Smile-Pillows Experience

Involuntary Grin while Meditating—A Sign

In my journal, I write all sorts of things about God, including my wish to see Him/Her smiling. I always thought that She must have been so busy working hard for humanity, and would have no time to smile, and I would imagine how it would be to see God smiling. Of course, this was just between my journal and me—nobody knew about it. Well, it seemed like She did! A year later, I painted the ceiling of my bedroom purple and the walls violet. While browsing in a store, I saw from afar two pillows the same colors as my room—violet and purple—with the word "SMILE" on them. That was shocking! I took them with me.

Lately, a smile from ear to ear would surface on my face during meditation. I did not pay much attention to it, as I thought it was just a reflex. But one night in November 2016, after praying Mother Mary's rosary, I heard:

> *"I am the Nameless One. I come in the name of God.*
> *I come in the name of Truth.*
> *Open your heart chakra.*
> *Expand it to receive my messages.*
> *I want to show you how to receive my messages."*

When I asked for a sign, the grin filled my lips! I realized it was He who had been making me smile during meditation. I said, "It is YOU!" And I heard:

> *"I want you to know that I am smiling at you."*

My body was trembling; goosebumps were all over it. The left side of my brain got cramped. I fell into a deep state of relaxation, and my head reclined on the head rest of the chair for a while. When I regained consciousness, I began crying and shaking in bliss. The excitement was great. A powerful flow of energy ran through me, and I did not know how to let it out! What an indescribable ecstasy. They were the most beautiful words I had ever heard.

I felt like floating in His rapture of love; I felt like crying! My Divine Nameless One came here to talk to me. What an honor. I believe in myself.

Within the Heart of God, I Am

I believe in miracles! I will never forget that statement. It will be with me forever. I will be using it every time I need a lift in my life. Thank you!

That night, I literally forced myself to get into bed. The next day, I woke up early and jumped out of bed thinking of Him. I thanked Him for coming to me in such a lovely way and was inspired to feel His support. Then I heard:

> *"I am the Nameless One. I am smiling.*
> *You are going to find messages waiting for you*
> *when you get out of the house."*
> *I asked, "How shall I know?"*
> *I heard Him say: "You will feel them.*
> *You will feel their scent."*

I adore You, beautiful Nameless One. When you come forth, my pain disappears, my anguish vanishes.

> *"I am the Nameless One. I come in the name of God.*
> *I want you to feel secure and loved at all times. No doubt."*
> *Me: "Yes, I understand.*
> *This is our relationship.*
> *I am honored."*

I went to the store. On my way back home, I received two potent lines that held my hand during the most painful times of my life.

> *"Nothing can be more powerful than a heart overflowing with love*
> *and gratitude.*
>
> *Do what seems to make less sense."*

The Hands of God in a Photograph

How did the hands of God appear in the sky? I tried to find an explanation, but the logical mind has to be put aside to understand the divine purpose of it. It is a remarkable sign that we are not alone. We are loved beyond measure. It was intended for you.

"Write the Memories of Your Life"
I Am That I Am

On the afternoon of November 7, 2018, I was trying to go deep into meditation, but a noisy chainsaw was bringing me in and out of my meditative state. I exclaimed out loud: *"Please stop that man from cutting trees!"*

Immediately afterwards, I sensed an amazing and indescribable love energy coming from my heart, indicating to me that a divine being was near. My body began to tremble, and I asked, *"Who are you?"* I heard, *"I Am that I Am."* Oh my God! My whole body shook! Electrical shocks were going up and down my whole being. My heart was beating fast. While doing my best to stay calm, I asked how I could be of greater service. I heard Him say, *"Write the memories of your life."*

Then I asked Him to put a hand on my heart. I felt it in my heart and also on my crown chakra. I felt extraordinary sensations of rapture, blissfulness, euphoria, and unconditional love like never before. It went beyond what words can describe. I could not contain my tears—tears of joy, tears of gratitude. I was speechless. My feelings of disbelief completely disappeared and were replaced with a deep sense of gratitude and appreciation. I began putting my writings together. Two days later, I was decluttering my phone pictures, and just when I was about to click the delete button on one photograph, I noticed those hands! The hands of God! Who else has the ability to place them in the sky?

Running Away from My Purpose?

During my time alone with the Divine, I have seen clearly how the obsession of gaining monetary stability had been inhibiting me from completely surrendering to my higher purpose. I had performed all sorts of activities to acquire the so-called financial freedom: taking unnecessary classes, struggling to start a new business, losing funds in an angel application, and others. However, nothing worked.

Why? Because those activities were pushing me away from my destiny. My destiny was to share my experiences with others. That was what God, as well as other Divine Beings had been telling me since 2014, but I kept ignoring it. Instead, I chose to stay in fear and tried more ways to obtain an income, doubting my real purpose and my heart's desire. When we live worrying about finances, we are not trusting our divine self. The real treasure is easy to achieve. But we are so addicted to drama, when something appears too easy and relaxed, we retract and go back to the misery that stress brings!

I have learned that when we follow our higher-self desires, abundance comes without drama.

My deepest desire is that my experience inspires you to get out of the survival mode for just a few minutes a day and connect with the power of your heart. Meditate on questions such as: How much joy do I have? Is my heart singing frequently? What steps am I taking to reach a state of enlightenment? If your answers don't make you smile, it is time to open your heart and live your own truth, even if it seems unreachable or absurd. Take daily steps to get there. Check Chapter V.

CHAPTER II
MYSTICAL EXPERIENCES AND PILGRIMAGES

A Divine Mother message opens this chapter, followed by some mystical experiences. Below you will find the very first photograph that led to a session that reconnected me with my divine Masters, as well as some pilgrimages stories.

"I am Divine Mother. I come in the name of truth;
I come in the name of Love.
I want you to learn the value of appreciation,
The value of gratitude—appreciate yourself,
Learn to trust yourself,
To love yourself,
To be yourself.
The veil has been lifted; you can see now.
The road ahead is clear for you to move on.
Move onto your destiny, your path.
Forget the worries; focus on yourself.
Never Underestimate the Power of Love."

The First Photograph that Opened the Door to My Awakening

On a sunny morning in April 2014, I felt the urge to photograph the sunrise from my room. Along with the natural scenario, I noticed a strange golden figure on the left of my phone's screen. It was similar to one of those Indigenous pieces found in burial tombs. The same symbol continued appearing for several days. Very intrigued by the apparition, I emailed the photograph to Dr. Norma Milanovich. She offered the opportunity to channel a session for me. I accepted it gladly.

The following is the transcription I made to the best of my ability from the recording session. This is what she channeled:

"*The voice of Oneness had told me when preparing for this reading that between lifetimes in your sacred contract you'd inquire for a hearing before Melchizedek, for you knew that at this time and space on your earthly journey you would need their guidance. But more than guidance, you would need encouragement to go forward and understand your own soul. You have seen yourself accelerate with ease and grace in many areas, but just when you have achieved a certain momentum and met certain goals, you've run out of steam. Your will decrease, and you don't have the same power and internal motivation anymore. Thus, in calculating your past, you looked into the future and determined that you would be faced with the same dilemma at precisely this time and space.*

You chose a time when it was harder and harder for you to move forward, to push through the resistance. It is like punching your way out of the veil when the journey becomes so sore and the resistance so strong that you begin to lose your footing and find yourself retreating even while you are advancing.

The ascended realms look at your contract and have chosen to send to you Master El Morya, Chohan of the first ray: the blue ray of truth, discipline, will, the right use of will, universal law, etc. They also have chosen to send forth Master Kuthumi, the universal teacher, the lord of love, grace and wisdom.

And Melchizedek himself has chosen to come forward at this time to guide you through what is called the final resistance, so that the point of your own arrow can pierce the veil, the shields around you, and help you begin a new journey, an accelerated journey upon a higher platform of light. This is what this lifetime for you is all about. It is not about relationships. This voice of oneness, their collective voice, are talking to me as your transcriber, your secretary, your liaison, if you will. Because that stuck energy from within is the point of resistance.

Now, these three masters, as they prepare to bring you to this arena, wish for you to know, to hear again, what was just revealed:

All resistance resides within you ...

Once you fully understand this, take ownership of it. Take the responsibility that comes from understanding this truth and move forward in the grace of God. Once understood, there will be nothing that can or will stop you in your path to achieving eternal life and receiving fully the grace of God.

So, I am asked right now to connect with your higher bodies and bring you to this sacred place abounding in the love and light of Christ. I gladly do so and, as I appear before you, I hold out my hand, and your higher bodies latch onto me as we move out into this other dimension of time and space. It is like we just step through a portal, an incredible universe literally aligned with the love of Venus. The colors in this environment are blue and green, the colors of our heart and throat chakra. You are wearing a magnificent flowing gold and white gown, and in your beauty, you stand there in the center of what appears to be a wooded area. There are trees, like on the Earth plane, and they are beautiful. It is like you are in a glen with beautiful flowers, pure, fresh, sparkling water, and the purest air you can ever imagine breathing.

I stepped back, for I am your witness, and as I do, I open up an area around you. Three masters appear: Ascended Master El Morya appears to your right, Melchizedek appears in front of you, and Ascended Master Kuthumi appears to your left. The three of them clasp their hands in front of them in position and bow to you. You do the same. This shows me that you understand the protocol of the higher agendas. Not only that, for I see your heart rejoice. You know these three masters well, not only through many lifetimes, but in your out-of-body experiences. They are your friends, your confidants, and you trust them.

On the Earth plane, most souls can lose their way momentarily by forgetting the higher laws and how to place, use and apply them in the proper perspective. You have been compromised in this lifetime, forgetting the power and commands you have used lifetime after lifetime, for eternity, like the sacred codes that always set you free and help to move you forward. You are now humbly asking them for assistance, so these three recognize you as a high commander in the light; they show you quickly some of your past lives where your greatness was shown with bravery, courage, wisdom, knowledge, helpfulness and complete devotion to God. In fact, I see that in one lifetime you were in a convent with St. Therese, who was called the Little Flower of Jesus. You were very much like her in that lifetime, aligned with principles of being literally the bride of Christ, so devoted to the spiritual way that you were noted in the minds and hearts of many. You were with her when she crossed over into the higher realms at a young age. In fact, you were one of her greatest teachers in helping her ascend to sainthood in that lifetime.

As you stand before these three and they show you the greatness of your soul lifetime after lifetime, they remind you once again to look inward for the answers you seek. There is nothing that is contained outside of you that you do not have the power to heal.

But always remember, dear one—and now this is Melchizedek speaking—always remember the words of Sananda 2,000 years ago when he walked the Earth plane and was asked on numerous occasions:' How do you perform the miracles that you do? How do you do what you do?' He always responded: 'Of me I do nothing. It is the Father within me that does it all.'

Melchizedek analyzes your own constitution, your chakra system. He has said to you that in the vicinity of your heart and throat there is a disconnection. He directs the energy from his hand directly at your basic chakra system of the seven main chakras—the red and yellow, green, blue, indigo and violet—and as he directs the energy there, he spins all the chakras in a clockwise direction. The detachment occurred in your auric field due to the thoughts and words of people that hurt your heart and made you exhausted and disappointed. You have allowed the chakra's flow of energy to be disrupted. Melchizedek restores you now to the perfect balance.

Melchizedek says that with every concern you experience in life labeled as a problem, concern, disappointment, or something you might consider even unconquerable, immediately remember that the universe and all the God force resides within you through the Father. Go inward; do not try to solve the problem yourself. Instead, offer it up to your Father, to Sananda, to the Holy Spirit, whose power sustains you, feeds you with light and endless love in every single concern you have. Learn to go inward and with humbleness say the following prayer:

> *'Oh, heavenly Father, my brother Jesus, beloved Holy Spirit, take this problem and fix it. This person who provides me with this challenge is upsetting my balance and blocking my path. I cannot see clearly, because I am weak. I cannot find the strength that you provide me to use. I need your help. I need your assistance now. I offer this problem up to you. Show me the way. Teach me what I need to do to be your arms and legs, your compassion, your absolute grace, your light shining the way on this new path called life.'*

And be calm; literally hold the light within your heart. Let the Holy Spirit work through you; stop the mouth from complaining, talking, reigniting the problem. Instead, get to know the power of your Father flowing through you, leading you through your accelerated destiny. Then step back and trust. Step out of the way and in silence watch the miracles that will happen.

You are already touching upon this power, but you did not connect the dots. You did not understand how you were able to achieve what you had achieved, because part of you was still thinking through your ego, from the ego's mind and the human embodied body. Begin to look at yourself differently now. Count your blessings on an ongoing basis every day by saying:

> *'Oh, heavenly Father, this is my challenge for today. Show me the way, fix it, solve the problem, so I am glorified in the eyes of God, climbing the summit of my own mountain called life.'*

Then wait, be silent, believe, trust. Once you master this on an ongoing basis, you will be one in this secured area between the fifth and sixth dimensions. And this great feeling of love that brought you here today will be yours.

You will merge with it. You will do the dance of life and bring it with you everywhere you go. It will take time, for it requires absolute trust. It requires an absolute knowingness, belief, and faith in your Father and faith in yourself to remember who you really are, to remember that you are the light of the world and extension of your brother Sananda, your Father, your Mother, that you have come to Earth to be a peacekeeper of the divine.

By holding counsel with your Father throughout day and night and offering every single little problem that you encounter up to your heavenly Father, you will begin to transform your life to such a degree that you will wonder some days if you are still a citizen of the Earth plane. You will see how you have ascended, yet you will walk around experiencing the third dimension in the same way that you experience it today.

It is your destiny—Melchizedek says—to become one with this aligned field. You have done it before, and you are destined to do it again. You cannot fight any battles any longer in the third dimension through your ego using its tools and the minds and egos of people around you.

You have graduated as of today into a higher arena, the arena of the mind surrounded by the love and light of God. Thus, you are entering a dimension of wizards who only understand the universal laws and the power of the great ones residing in other dimensions of time and space. You are already returning home. It is futile for you to discuss relationships one by one at this point, for you no longer reside in this dimension. This attunement by your own sacred contract is to be used as an acceleration into your mind through your heart. El Morya is present today. He has offered to work with you for the next nine days and nights to strengthen your willpower, and you are asked to merge with his essence consciously each day. Ask him for his strength, his will, his perfect knowingness of the law, and ask that this be left within you so that your own self-discipline becomes stronger and you are no longer deterred by morals or anyone around you.

Keep the focus only on yourself. This does not mean you will become self-centered in a negative way. Place your focus in your inner plane, which is the God force residing within you. Rejoice and relax. Stay in an alpha state of consciousness. Feel the love and light of God flowing through you, knowing that all problems—especially with relationships, but all problems in general—will be fixed by your Father in the grace of God. Therefore, do not dwell on them. Only tend to the details that need to be completed and ask for guidance. Let God show you the way. Hold that perfect image of the Christ within you. Let it guide you.

After the nine days, Ascended Master Kuthumi will be working with you in developing your mind to understand what must come with the next phase of this attunement in the dream state. He will guide you for three months. Every night you must ask him, before falling asleep, to open you to receive the new codes in your DNA. These codes will be aligning with your own RNA and nucleon within you to extend the strands of DNA that are destined to receive these higher codes, future instructions, and data.

This is the time for rebirth, for growth, and to rejoice. 'Our daughter,' Melchidezek says, 'You have come home. You have come home to dwell in the house of the Lord and yet remain the unencumbered, simple person that you are and who will change at an accelerated rate should you follow this guidance in the letter of the Lord. This is your time to move forward with power, to break the resistance that tries to hold you back. All you need to do is continue to direct your focus inward, to meet the God force within you, to open up your channels and allow the grace of God to flow through you. This is your time. This is your destiny, and you must consider yourself to be launched as of today, in this moment of time/space.'

They placed you now in a Merkaba of light, the vehicle of God. There is a tetrahedron duplicated above and below. The two sides begin to spin, pulling forth the purity that you command, supporting your chakra system and preparing a perfect path for you to follow. This is indeed a day to rejoice, for it is like your birthday, the first day of the rest of your life. You will remain in this Merkaba for the nine days of this attunement with El Morya.

Upon being released, you will be changed and then turned over to Master Kuthumi. He will guide and show you the way. Your Christ-Self is reset during this Easter season that just passed, and the light of God now directs your path.

I see and hear now the Angelic Realm coming around, chanting and putting up a barrier of protection around you. I hear them saying: 'Kadoish, Kadoish, Kadoish, Adonai Tsevayoth, Kadoish, Kadoish, Kadoish Adonai Tsebayoth, Kadoish, Kadoish, Kadoish, Adonai Tsevayoth. So be it, and so it is. It is done.'
End of session.

After I received this channeled session, no matter how many times I listened to it, I did not understand why they were saying those things to me. Many times, I even thought they were mistaken about the subject (me). I ended up ignoring it and continued my life as usual. Only five years later did I realize its power and the love coming through. As I read it again, tears of gratitude poured down my face. I learned that Ascended Masters are beings who lived on this planet many years ago. Because during those lifetimes they reached a high state of consciousness, they don't need to incarnate again. Nevertheless, they continue assisting humanity from the etheric and higher levels.

A Blue Bird Came to Me

Once in North Carolina, I wandered in the woods for a while. When I returned to the vehicle, I saw from a distance a little blue bird standing by the car door. It really seemed like he was waiting for me. I kept approaching the car, and he stayed still. I kneeled down to see if it was real; he was, and he actually seemed very relaxed. Surprisingly, he allowed me to grab him. Immediately, my intention was to capture the moment forever in a photograph, but my phone was on the opposite side and the door was closed. I said, "*Please let me take a picture of us.*" Amazingly, I was able to walk around the car, open the door, bend over, grab my phone, and take a few pictures! As if that were not enough, he allowed me to kiss him! Minutes later, when the car door closed abruptly, he flew away. Incredible! I still have to look at the pictures to remind myself that I was not dreaming.

On another day, I heard a bird singing very loudly. I went outside to investigate and saw that it was a cardinal. When he acknowledged my presence, he came down one branch and I heard: *"Your prayers have been heard."* I had a rapture moment because in the preceding days I had been praying for a miracle, and indeed it had manifested.

I would like to add that when I was a little girl, I attended the 4th grade in a small town surrounded by nature. I used to walk alone in the woods, and while listening to the birds chirping, I asked God with tears in my eyes to allow the birds to talk to me. I can now say that my pleas have been granted. How grateful I am.

The Animal Kingdom Helped a Missing Boy in North Carolina

On Tuesday, January 22, 2019, looking for the weather report on my phone, I saw on the news that a three-year-old boy was missing. Surprisingly, the event had happened about six hours away (or 6 miles?) from my cabin in North Carolina. They added that the little boy was playing outside his grandmother's backyard with other kids, and all but he went back inside.

I was so touched by this tragedy, imagining the level of desperation his family was going through. I took the case on like my own and began praying Mother Mary's rosary for an Ascended Humanity on his behalf, while following the case two or three times a day. The next day, the news reported: *"The FBI, along with a host of local departments and volunteers searched for the boy amid heavy rain, temperatures in the twenties, and strong winds."* I grew very concerned and pleaded with Mother Mary to intercede with the animal kingdom and set guardians to keep him warm, especially during the night.

Earlier Thursday, the sheriff's office described the search area as dangerous: *"The terrain is treacherous. Areas are flooded and filled with sinkholes; even the trained searchers are having trouble navigating safely."*

That night I tried to fall asleep, but something did not let me. I could sense energies around me. It was overwhelming. I got up twice to clear the space. Finally, I fell asleep, only to wake up again at 1:30 am. I checked the news, and he had been found! I wept in joy. I realized that the angels were trying to tell me that he would be found that night.

The police broadcasted the following: "*The missing boy was found calling for his mother about a quarter of a mile away, forty to fifty yards deep into the woods. He was soaking wet, cold, and tangled in thorn bushes. Rescuers waded through nearly waist-deep water to get to the toddler. How did he get there, and how did he stay alive?*"

A few days later I read: "*A three-year-old boy who was found alive in the woods of eastern North Carolina after he went missing for two days said he spent time with a bear.*" His aunt called her nephew's safety a "miracle" and said: "*God sent a friend to keep him safe.*"

The mother gave authorities the same report, that he had a friend in the woods that was a bear. Police said bears are common in the area, but they thought the comment was more "cute" than factual.

Aside from a few scratches, the boy was found in good health and was reunited with his family. His family said he was in good spirits, eating Cheetos, and watching *Paw Patrol*.

It was delightful to confirm that the animal kingdom hears our pleas and really takes part in our lives. My heart sings in gratitude. Thank you, Mother Mary, Mother Nature, angels and, of course, animal kingdom! Animals are blessings. Use them, include them in your prayers—they are here to help us.

Alaska Whales, A Show of Joy

In Alaska it is common to see the humpback whales. They are powerful swimmers that have distinctly robust shapes and are predominantly black with white on the throat, belly, flippers and flukes.

During an Alaskan cruise I was on, many passengers bragged about seeing a whale. I hadn't seen any. One morning while walking on the treadmill and contemplating the majesty of the ocean in front of me, I found myself saying: "*Where are they? Why I haven't seen any? Please, God, show me a whale!*"

After lunch and back in the room, I waited on the balcony, hoping to see one. Forty-five minutes passed and nothing happened. I stood up to return to the room. However, as soon as I grabbed the door handle, I looked back and my heart jumped! A whale was exhaling air through her blowhole far away! I screamed in joy, grabbed the video camera and waited for her to come closer. My amazement went overboard when I saw not just one but dozens of them approaching my balcony. The enthusiasm was so great that I abandoned the idea of recording and stared at them in a stupor. As they get closer, they put on a show of acrobatic displays, using their tails to propel themselves through the water and sometimes through the air, landing with a tremendous splash, showing their flukes. They totally surrounded the L-shaped balcony. It seemed like they were on a mission. I did not know which side to look at, so I ran around trying to catch it all at once. What a remarkable experience! A great proof that our prayers are indeed heard. I will never get tired of thanking God for this miraculous gift.

A Golden Bird Shape in the Sky

While on a Caribbean cruise in December 2014, I felt the urge to go to the balcony. Once there, I detected a huge, golden bird shape far away in the sky. I grabbed my camera zoomed in and took a photograph. I was impressed with the perfection of the bird's shape, so golden and brilliant. Even though I thought of it for a while, the image just dissipated in my mind. Months later, while doing these drawings in 2015, I received the following:

"I am that bird—I just wanted to get your attention."

When I heard those words, a great loving filled me completely. The right side of my brain numbed for a nanosecond, my body shivered. I was perplexed. I stopped drawing for a while to recover. Then I wrote the following:

"Divine God, Source of Love
How can You be so divine?
I can't grasp that concept.
I ask my heart,
But I don't sense an answer."
Wait, I heard:
"It is unexplainable, for it is not a concept the mind can discern;
Only the heart can feel it,
Even though it's not a feeling!"

Angels Holding the Plane

My wonderful granddaughter, almost six years old, agreed to travel alone, to spend time with me. On the way to the airport to drop her off, I filled everything she was going to be in contact with, including the plane, the crew members, and the passengers, with divine light, calling upon the angels to take care of them. A remarkable event happened the last time: while watching the plane take off, I saw angels holding it! I cried at that moment and am still amazed and grateful to them for listening to my prayers. My purpose in sharing this is to make you aware that angels exist and are ready to help us. They listen to our prayers and are always with us. Call on them for assistance.

A Little Lost Soul in My Home

During the summer of 2017, my granddaughter, who was about five years old, came to visit me for a few days. After her departure, I kept sensing the presence of a child playing by my bed and preventing me from sleeping. I was confused and thought that something might be happening to my granddaughter. I called her mom frequently, asking about her, but the answer was always that she was fine. It came into my awareness that when my little one was visiting, we had played with a small ball in the living room when all of a sudden, the ball disappeared! We never found it. I dismissed it and did not worry about it again. Then a few days later, a highly advanced clairvoyant friend of mine came to visit. While showing her around, she noticed something out of place and asked me: *"Have you just done a session on someone?"* The answer was no. She added, *"Because there is someone here on the massage table."* She came closer to find out that there was a little girl there. She said that she and her parents had been killed in South America a long time ago. She had come with my granddaughter, liked my place, and stayed. It all made sense. She was the little girl I had been perceiving playing with a ball beside my bed; but when I cleared the space, she did not go into the light because she did not understand English!

I was sad that she had been lost for a long time. My heart cried in silence. My friend called for the assistance of the Brotherhood of the Light and the angels to assist her to go into the light. They sent a seat in the shape of a swing to take her in a comfortable way; she felt how soft it was and got on immediately. (As I am writing these words, I am looking through my window and see three beautiful butterflies putting a show on for me—it could be their soul saying hello. My heart melts with compassion and joy.) I learned a lot from this experience. I thought that the language did not matter in the astral realm. It was rewarding to know that she reunited with her family at last.

A Bird's Visitor

When I moved to Port St. Lucie, Florida, a beautiful red cardinal came pecking at my window and peering into the bedroom every day. It seemed that he was trying to get my attention, flying back and forth swiftly between the window and the tree. He would not leave until I came to see him. One day, I decided to greet him, and I asked: *"Do you sing? I have never heard you singing."* Well, the next day I was in my bedroom when I heard a bird singing. I ran out to the balcony, thinking it must have been a new one, but to my surprise it was the cardinal. As soon as he saw me, he flew closer to me. It was like he was saying, *"Hey, it was me. I can sing!"*

Another day, I asked him: *"Do you have a family? Why are you always alone?"*

A few days later, I heard his tapping at the window and ran to my bedroom. When the bird saw me, he flew to a branch where a small red female cardinal was waiting for him. He wanted me to see his mate! I was amazed by this incredible and joyful gift. It lifted my spirit in a powerful way.

Another day, while sitting on my balcony and rewarding myself by watching the birds coming and going, I noticed that a new red one, who was much smaller than the others, had arrived. I focused on my heart, intending to communicate with his consciousness, and asked him to be within me. I clearly heard: *"I AM IN YOU."* It was a moment of divine rapture. I stayed with my eyes closed for a while, enjoying that heavenly moment. Animals play an important role in our lives; I am sure they are aware of the joy their presence gives us. Let's take a moment to bless our animal kingdom.

Colorful Clouds—Love and Support from the Sky

This event happened during a very uncomfortable situation. I was a passenger in a car. We were driving on Interstate Highway 95 in Florida. The density was so intense inside the vehicle that I was not even able to speak a word. When I looked up to the sky, I distinguished three small clouds. It was like one on top of the other, like little pillows. Each one had a different color: blue, pink, and green—very pale tones, but easy to recognize. I yelled in joy, pointing out to them. The driver tried to look at them but could not see them. Needless to say, the event raised my vibration instantaneously.

A few months later, as soon as I walked into a consignment store, I looked to my right and saw three little angels: one blue, one pink, and the other green. They were the same pale colors as the clouds I had seen in Florida. I bought them and keep them with me. I am grateful to the angels for being around me constantly.

A Bird's Convention by My Deck

One day while standing by the veranda of my cabin, I began reciting the Lord's Prayer with my eyes closed. Unbeknownst to me, I had an audience up in the trees. After a while, I opened my eyes to witness at least seven cardinals and mockingbirds listening to my appeals. Stunned, I did not move for a while. I thanked them for their support. Then they flew away. Are they angels? Somebody told me that cardinals are from the Angelic Realm. What do you think?

A Rattle Snake

While looking for the cabin of my dreams, I visited one located at the top of a mountain; completely away from the world and surrounded by a beautiful landscape. The first thing I found on the porch floor were two beautiful feathers of the big one on my forearm. I kept them and use them as a tool for healings.

I went out to explore the territory, for a moment I stopped and what would not be my surprise when I look down and next to my right sandal was a coiled rattlesnake apparently sleeping. I screamed in terror and ran away, in my flight I turned my face to look at her to discover that she hadn't even moved!

Days later I confirmed that it was a rattlesnake because a neighbor had a dissected one on his property. I am very grateful that she kept sleeping.

Chemtrails in Sedona and in Florida

When I moved to Sedona in 2015, I noticed that there were tons of chemtrails being sprayed each day, almost exactly above my dwelling. I was inspired to ask for Mother Mary's assistance in dissolving or neutralizing them. We started working. I visualized filling with divine light every person and machine involved in their development, starting with those who signed the approval, those transporting, disseminating, producing the chemicals, as well as the plane itself. It was meaningful to see how they had basically disappeared from the area when I left Sedona and Port St. Lucie, Florida. I remembered friends in Sedona also noticing that they were gone. Two beautiful friends were pointing out their absence when they visited the area.

This fact made me believe that together we can transmute anything into light and love. Mother Mary is waiting for your call. Let's work together to empower a web of harmony around our beautiful planet.

A Bird's Love Story

On my deck I had the opportunity to see and enjoy different types of birds that came for food or were attracted by the flowers or plants of the place.

Once, I repeatedly saw two little birds going back and forth. I was delighted to see that they were building a nest right inside one of my hanging plants. Days later, I was passing by when I noticed the bird hatching the eggs and, to my astonishment, the male bringing her food while she was confined! I never thought of that behavior in birds. It is like when a woman has given birth and the male, or her family takes care of her. This bird was coming to check on her many times a day! I felt so privileged to witness the beauty and perfection of Mother Nature. Once the babies were born, one watches them while the other looks for food. When they were ready to fly, the joy was palpable—not just the parents' delight, but many other birds surrounded the nest singing, chirping, going back and forth, celebrating the arrival of more birds on Earth!

An event that stunned me was the fact that when the little ones hatched, a flower bloomed from the almost-dead plant they had used for their nest. So many miracles Mother Nature embraces.

Divine Love

One time while I was waiting at a crowded bus stop with others, we could not avoid seeing a father reprimanding his child. Sadly, we noticed that when the boy tried to get close to his father he was rejected. The mother was watching them while standing up against a column. She did not intervene nor give any attention to the child. The boy then stood far away from both his father and his mother.

Inspired by The Divine Mother, I began pouring energy of Love onto all three freely without any expectations. After only a few minutes, it was rewarding to see that the father went to hug the mother. She was facing the child and extended her hand out to him to join them.

My heart rejoiced when I saw all three hugging one another!

Divine Love works marvelously in any situation. Begin using it as a tool for peace and unity. There are times when we all need to be reminded that love is the easiest way to heal.

Michael Jackson

I would like to share that Michael Jackson (the singer) appeared to me a couple of times during meditation. I could acknowledge he was in a safe place of light. The first time he gave me an encouraging message about my path. Months later, after I read a comment that his daughter posted in a social media stating that it was time to transcend all judgments about her father and let it go, he appeared again showing me his daughter and his youngest son. I sensed that he was asking me to fill them with divine Light. I poured the light and love of the divine Mother on his three children.

While polishing this book for publication, I learned that his second apparition came forth by the time his daughter, according to the media, had attempted suicide. I came to the realization that he must have been concerned about her. I was deeply touched by this act of love and specially honored to be of service.

Soul Retrieval at the Hualapai Indian Reservation

Great Canyon, Arizona

Soon after my arrival in Sedona, Arizona, I noticed an uncomfortable pain in the back of my heart that would not go away. Looking for the cause of it, I used Dr. Joe Dispenza's meditation with the intention to receive an answer. I went out of my body to see myself as a man living in an Indian settlement at the bottom of the Great Canyon. Another tribe attacked us, and my family was killed. Also, a poisoned arrow hit me in the back of my heart, causing my death.

I asked: *"How can I heal this?"* I was guided to take the arrow out and slowly ground it in Mother Earth, filling it with divine light and forgiveness for those who had shot it at me. Then I made a circle in the sky that symbolized divine light pouring over my tribe and protecting them from any other invasion or attempts to disrupt their lives.

This meditation was my inspiration to take a trip to or near the base of the Grand Canyon. Since there was no availability at any of the accommodations there, I ended up near the Colorado River at the Grand Canyon Resort, which is owned and operated by the Hualapai tribe in Peach Springs, Arizona. It is situated on the longest stretch of highway left of the original historic Route 66. It is the primary starting point for travelers looking to explore the raw Grand Canyon landscape.

I left the house early on Wednesday, May 4, 2016. I had a nice drive and stayed in Williamstown for one night, where I found the people to be extremely nice and caring.

The next day, I took Route 66 to Peach Springs. As soon as I took that highway, I sensed an energy change, and by the time I got to the lodge, the energy had worsened. The check-in time was at 3:00 p.m. I arrived at 2:45 p.m. When I asked the receptionist to allow me to check-in fifteen minutes early, she refused. The staff was mostly robot-like—nobody really smiled, and even if they tried, they could not. Once in my room, I blessed and cleared the space. Since it was early, I decided to drive around to check out the surroundings. However, as soon as I got into my car, I heard: "*Go back to your room and don't go out.*"

I did that quickly, but as soon as I entered my room, I began feeling ill. I thought a bath with sea salt might help, but the sickness became overwhelming, forcing me to lie down.

The energy in the room was dense. I thought I might need to do another clearing, but my energy was gone. I could only shout, "*Archangel Michael, I am exhausted, and I don't know what's going on. Please help me clear this space!*" I noticed Archangel Michael to the right side of the bed. That was the first time I noticed him with my naked eyes.

As time passed, my illness worsened. I could hardly move. It was like I had a knife in my throat. My body got very sore, and a terrible headache began to attack me. It is hard to describe how ill I was. Little by little, things were getting worse. Then, I became paralyzed. I felt like I was attached to the bed by invisible ties. I tried to get up several times without success. I opened my eyes wider and wider, but I couldn't see anything. It took me a while to realize that I was blind.

All I could see were rays of light going out of or coming into my eyes. I couldn't be sure. My vision was gone, and I was shaking! My body was trembling in pain! I remember praying that I would be able to get up the next morning. All sorts of things began to cross my mind, such as: *How is my daughter going to know where I am? I did not tell her exactly where I was heading to. And even if she knew, she wouldn't be able to come and take my car. We have no family here at all.* Finally, with no energy left, I surrendered. I stopped trying to get up or understand what was going on. I just knew I was in a battle. I fell unconscious.

During those two days, I was able to get up in a robotic mode to cancel the rafting reservation I had made when I arrived at the lodge. I went back to bed and fell unconscious day and night until 7:30 a.m. two days later. At that time, I finally managed to gather the necessary energy to get up, grab my stuff, and leave. Once in my car, I heard: *"Drive. Do not even look back."* I followed the instructions and drove straight home.

Reflection

Could the tribe I'd visited been the one that hurled the poisoned arrow? Maybe. The point is, by going through this experience, that debt was healed. The pain had disappeared.

By the time I drove near my territory, a wonderful sense of compassion, forgiveness and gratitude filled my being. I felt great relief. Painful episodes from my past transpired before my eyes like a video, except now those events meant nothing. There was no judgment and no negative emotions at all. A great sense of peace dwelled within me. I had recovered a part of my soul.

Further in the book, I mention a soul retrieval that assisted me to heal from and recover those parts of my soul that might have been lost. They have brought a lot of clarity and tranquility.

PILGRIMAGES

The John of God Experience—Brazil

I would say that Mother Mary inspired me to visit John of God's healing center in Abadiania, Brazil. Three years later, I discovered the reasons. Here are the details.

Because I was living in Sedona, Arizona, the best route was to fly from Phoenix to Miami and then Miami to Brazil. I was picked up by the SuperShuttle at around 3:00 a.m. and sat in the first seat by the window. A man took the seat near me. Between the two of us, there was my briefcase with $600 cash to pay my guides in Brazil.

During the route to the airport I felt asleep. At the Phoenix airport I took the flight to Miami. Once there, I reached for my wallet to make a payment to find out that my money was gone. I was shocked, and the image of that man came into my awareness immediately. I was saddened. I tried to reach the shuttle people with the hope that I was wrong and that they had the money, but there was no response. I left a message, and they never called back. I sat on a bench and cried. I went to the bathroom to calm myself down. I decided to let it go and to send divine light into the situation and all those involved. I would not allow this event to ruin my enthusiasm.

When checking in, another situation came forth. I had bought the ticket with my married name, but now my maiden name was on my driver's license. It took a while to straighten that out. I wondered if those were signs that the voyage would become stressful at some point.

The House of John of God- Brazil

My guides picked me up at the airport and took me to a small but clean hotel. The staff was very nice, and the food was fantastic. Later, we went to the waterfall located behind the house. The energy was very powerful there. The next day, we went to the house to meet John in person. There were long lines of people waiting to meet him with their personal requests. Once you were in front of him, you had the option to make a request. I chose assistance to fulfill my mission on Earth. He ordered meditation. I joined others in a room who were seating on plain benches and listening to someone who recited prayers in English and in Portuguese. I stayed there for about four hours.

On the second day, we had the chance to meet him in person again and to make another request. This time, I decided to ask for help with dissolving a nodule on my thyroid. He ordered psychic surgery that was done in the afternoon. As before, I was taken to a special room where many people sat on wooden benches with their eyes closed. Thirty minutes later, we were told to go to the hotel room and avoid contact with television, computers, or people for twenty-four hours. We were to come back for a final check-out the day after that.

During those twenty-four hours of seclusion, Divine Mother Mary showed me that I was to bring a bouquet of pink roses to him. After the twenty-four hours had elapsed, I left the room and went to different places looking for the pink roses until I found twenty-four beautiful ones. I also learned how to say "I love you" in Portuguese. Once in front of him, I extended the flowers and said, "*Eu te amo.*" Instantly, the whole room brightened exponentially, and his face changed completely. I saw a great deal of peace in his eyes. I did not say anything else and left. That was my only contact with him, and now I have been advised to share it with you.

Later, I received confirmation that Mother Mary was indeed who had come forth when I handed the bouquet of pink flowers to him. She wanted to bring the Divine Feminine Force to that place. I guess she knew that sad events would take place in the very near future.

Three Years Later

Now, three years later, I can go back in time and see perfection in bringing him pink flowers and the meaning that those flowers had on him as well as on the place. New events related to that visit have emerged, and here they are.

For some reason, I did not have this story in my papers when organizing my documents to write this book. However, one early morning as soon as I awoke, I heard, "*Write about John of God.*" Later that day when I checked the computer, the first thing that appeared was the news that the lady who had denounced John of God for running baby farms had killed herself while hiding in Spain. I had no idea about those charges. I was perplexed.

I immediately connected that I had been crying without reason, unable to sleep, and with an unexplainable sense of sadness over me. I realized that I was feeling her sorrow.

Since the voice had told me to write about it, I reluctantly began doing so. However, the coldness in the room was extreme. Low temperatures had been hitting my town, but this coldness was dreadful and impossible to ignore. It was getting into my bones, forcing me to stop writing, and urging me to go deeper to find the reason.

I sensed many entities in my place. As usual, I did a clearing and it felt better, but just for a while. While making lunch, I perceived that there was more to do related to John of God's issue. I discerned that the lady who had taken her own life a few days before was looking for help. She was in my house. She had tried to talk to me, but unfortunately, I couldn't decipher her message.

Therefore, I began a session and asked the angels to take her into the light, to cross the bridge to freedom. Convinced that such event was resolved, I went back to my writing. That night I could not sleep. I sensed presences again. I left my mattress and sat in the living room, focusing in my heart. I saw her again asking for help but not just for her—she had brought many women who had been stuck in the astral level, wandering around. There were many, and they were young. I could hardly handle it without crying. I asked for divine assistance. Angels and Mother Mary came forth, and we opened a vortex of light and they went in peace. A singular vision took place. Many angels formed a spiral of beautiful light and surrounded the lady who had brought them to me. They took her to heaven. She was, in fact, a saint, an angel who cared and suffered for all those women. I blessed her and the rest of the ladies.

Nevertheless, the day after, my place was full of more people. This time many men came forth. I began the clearing process and asked them to go in peace and love, but they refused. They wanted me to hear their complaints. They wanted justice, but for what? I had no idea. I could sense they were good people with good intentions. I explained to them about my inability to hear the dead. I could only assist them in going in peace and love with the angels and the Christ. After trying for a while, these men accepted what I said and went with the angels. It was painful to see others' pain, but at least they are in good hands now. I am not a judge. I just happened to be in the middle of this situation and was told to share it with my readers. Every day I learn more about love after life, and that life does not end with what we call death. It is a beginning.

Meditation after the Event

The next day, I was inspired to do a massive healing for Brazil. Thus, I called for the presence of Mother/Father God, the Angelic Realm, the Ascended Master, and our Galactic Family. We flew over Brazil, opening many vortices of light and love. We invited all lost souls to go into the light, to freedom. There were countless souls who went into the vortices of light. We expanded the force of love all over Brazil and filled Brazilians' hearts with a pink rose as a symbol of the Divine Mother's presence. Then we opened the rose in love, compassion, peace and light. It was a powerful meditation. I am humbled to be of service. The greatest reason for sharing this is to inspire you, beautiful reader, to do the same in any place you feel love and peace are needed.

Camino De Santiago Pilgrimage - Spain

(Also known as The Way of St. James). We started in the magical city of Barcelona and continued to Monserrat. This is a traditional starting point for the Camino de Santiago. We walked along the Magical Mountain of Montserrat and continued through San Jaume to the Ermita of San Miguel. Then we continued on to Jaca, where we visited the Monastery of San Juan de la Peña. Jaca is known as the pearl of the Pyrenees and offers a blend of spectacular nature sites in Spain which are hard to beat. We headed to Zariquiegi, to the Church of Santa María de Eunate, one of the most impressive churches in Spain. From there we went to Logrono, Burgos, and Leon, visiting many cathedrals we found on the way.

The most notable was Leon's Cathedral Gothic Temple of Light, located in northwest Spain. León Cathedral is a French-style, Gothic cathedral built in the thirteenth century over the ruins of Roman baths. These pools were an important part of daily life of ancient Rome. The intricately carved portals, glorious rose windows, one of the oldest choirs in the country, and beautiful sculptures, such as the Virgen de la Esperanza, are just a few of the cathedral's many striking features.

Also impressive is the imposing Templar Castle in Ponferrada. It is enormous; the architecture is stunning, and it is an absolute fortress. The castle was named after the Knights Templar, who protected the town in the twelfth century.

Finally, we arrived at Santiago de Compostela. The impressive cathedral allegedly holds the remains of Saint James. Then we walked to Finisterre on a beautiful path with an enchanted forest, medieval towns and gorgeous countryside. I fell in love with Spain's scenery and the kindness of its people.

Here are some of my important experiences while walking the Camino a Santiago trail.

The Mount of Forgiveness

There is a place called the Mount of Forgiveness where it's said pilgrims visit to leave what they no longer want to carry. At the top of the Mount of Forgiveness is a metalwork sculpture dedicated to pilgrims' past, present and future. It depicts pilgrims struggling against the wind on their way to Santiago. The pose of the figures is rather accurate, for the mountain is windswept and desolate. Inscribed on the sculpture, interpreted into English, it says: "*This path is where the wind and the stars meet.*"

Preparing for this trip, I decided to bring some earrings with the intention of leaving them as a symbol of renunciation and forgiveness for what they had represented in my life. That little gesture made a great impact in my life. It made me feel free from oppression.

Also, when we started walking towards the mount, our guide asked us to talk to a stranger about the importance of forgiveness. Upon arrival, I found a girl selling lemonade, and a young man buying it. When I told them the story, the man eagerly volunteered to listen to me. We went to an isolated corner, and I began talking. Minutes later, he began weeping uncontrollably, because his girlfriend had just left him for someone else and he was too mad to even think of forgiveness.

I guided him into a very relaxed state of mind. Since he did not believe in Divine Mother or in God, I asked him to invoke the power of his own heart. After a while, he was smiling and grateful. I would like to add that I often find people who do not want to hear the name of God but believe in the power of love. For me, that is interchangeable, because God is Love and Love is God. I continued with the healing or counseling without giving too much importance to that detail. I am convinced that God lives in the heart, and a name is not so relevant.

Archangel Michael's Golden Boots

When I got tired of walking, I called upon the presence of Archangel Michael to let me use his golden boots. I visualized myself putting them on and, *voilà*, something amazing happened! I began running instead of walking and was the first one to reach the final point most of the time.

At the end of each walk, before I joined the group, I secluded myself to pray Mother Mary's rosary for an Ascended Humanity, asking for a different cause every day. That provided me with great peace as I sensed her divine presence constantly.

It was an inspirational experience. I walked mostly alone, connecting with my own self, meditating about my dreams, my past, present and near future.

Before the trip, Mother Mary came forth and suggested to me that I drop a rose at the end of the way. I did it. She has been my inspiration and confidante. At the very end, by the tomb of St. James in Santiago de Compostela, I could not contain my tears—some connection was there that made me cry in silence.

On our bus I changed seats to initiate conversation with a lovely Spaniard girl. She was confiding in me her doubts and fears as well as her urge to learn how to open her heart. I offered her my assistance, and she accepted. I advised her to breathe and focus in her heart center. A few minutes later, she started crying and said, *"This is exactly what I was looking for! I just did not know how to do it."* She opened up and expressed all her anguish; we sent that pain into the light. Her expression changed noticeably. She felt happier and grateful. She shared that she had found a card that morning saying that she would find what she needed in order to move forward with her life purpose. Divine Mother was present in her life.

During our travels we stopped by the Monastery of San Juan De la Peña, which is a gem of the Middle Ages. This photograph captured an immense white light on the roof of the place.

Himalayan Trekking

Ancient Attraction

When I saw the announcement online for this trip, my heart opened considerably. The photographs of the scenic views made me sign up. Actually, they brought me to tears. Something inside me recognized that energy. During the months prior to the trip, my soul was nurtured just by visualizing myself there.

Months later, I met the trekking group in Kathmandu, Nepal. We shopped and mingled a few days before the adventure began.

We hiked the Annapurna Circuit, walking about 20 kilometers daily. This path holds a fascinating land of biodiversity—the scenic grandeur making it a popular trekking destination. The feeling of a mighty presence while passing through this territory is unequivocal. I felt connected the whole time. Besides that, I was blessed to walk along with a magnificent group. It was actually a particular combination of angels and masters like I have never seen before, including the packers and guides.

The Experience

Pokhara was the gateway of our trekking adventure; from there we reached Tikhedhunga. Afterward, we walked on a wide, stone-paved trail passing waterfalls and bamboo forest. The trek drops like a staircase and then traverses high above the river. We walked about 9.6 kilometers the first day.

I would like to give credit to Bipan Khadka, who took that awesome picture of the Himalayan Nepal. He was one of the persons in the group of packers. He is currently a guide for Navigator Nepal Company.

The next day, we went from Tikhedhunga to Ghorepani, crossing a couple of bridges on a trail that then ascends on never-ending steep stairs. Some state that there are 3,300 steps; others believe there are 3,767. For sure I did not want to count them—it felt like thousands. Someone claimed to have counted them and stated that there were over 7,000. I personally considered it the most difficult part of all. We added 9.4 kilometers.

The next day, we rose before dawn to offer sunrise prayers at Poon Hill, which is one of the best Himalayan viewpoints in Nepal. The view is spectacular and well worth the hour-long early morning climb along stone stairs through rhododendron forest. It is the absolute highlight of the journey. At

10,230 feet in elevation, it provides 360-degree views of the surrounding, snow-capped mountains. A very convenient kiosk stands there selling coffee and hot chocolate.

A Remarkable Encounter— The Divine Feminine

Then we began our trek from Ghorepani Poon Hill to Tatopani. I got immersed in the beauty of the land, feeling Mother Nature's nectar decanting into my consciousness. Singing the Hail Mother, I entered into a spectacular valley surrounded by enormous mountains and misty views of terraced villages.

Hiking along a parallel ridge—surely one of the most scenic hikes I have ever taken—I sensed an energy change in the area. That is when in the distance I spotted an iconic figure on the far mountains. I grabbed my iPhone from my backpack and zoomed it in as much as possible to capture the image of a figure encrypted on a peak of a mountain: The Sacred Feminine was there! See the breathtaking proof.

During lunch, I showed the picture to the group. I intended to send it to everyone, but for some reason only one person received it. We finished lunch and continued walking. As we began, I asked one of the packers to carry my jacket with my iPhone in it. I must confide that a little voice inside me told me to take the phone out, but I bizarrely ignored it. I wish I knew why! We continued trekking, and when we reached the dinner meeting point, I noticed that the packer was not there. Minutes later, he came to me with a very gloomy expression on his face to communicate that he had lost my jacket. I thought it was impossible and tried to stay in control. He was so distraught that I comforted him and did my best to let it go. Of course, it was very traumatic to lose my phone/camera in a foreign country, especially in the Himalayas. I was in distress; the episode robbed me of my peace for a while. That day we walked 13.3 km.

Divine Lesson

Interestingly, the group's intention was to embody Omnipresence to assist the transcendence of the collective trauma and belief system of the "victim and victimizer" program. These are universal patterns of behavior that, once discovered, help us better understand ourselves and our place in the world. I appreciate the assistance of the group in helping me to realize that the previous pair of events—the apparition of the Divine Mother and the loss of my iPhone—were an initiation for me. At a subconscious level, I had chosen to lose my iPhone exactly after I had captured Her apparition.

Even though the first event was joyful and the second painful, they were interconnected. It was like I had chosen pain after joy, denying myself more joy by losing my iPhone. That pattern had appeared before, but my conscious mind kept ignoring it—until then. It provided me with a great opportunity to face it, heal it, and let it go.

By being consciously aware of my decisions, I transcended the experience of victim/victimizer, stopped blaming others, and took responsibility for my own creations. It was a great teaching.

Then we went from Tatopani to Ghasa, following the Kali Gandaki River that flows under the deep gorge in between two mountain tops with a very interesting suspension bridge we had to cross. It was a pleasure to enjoy the continuing Namaste and smiles on each local person through the villages. We walked 11.7 km.

From Ghasa to Marpha, the walk distance was twenty-two kilometers. This trail follows the Kaligandaki River through a narrow gorge with steep climbs passing through traditional Thakali villages. They have kept its narrow, paved alleys, passageways and flagstone streets. Marpha and its residents are of the ethnic group Thakalis. Their wool goods are famous and taken from yak hair, which is rich and cozy. I took advantage and obtained a great variety of them. We continued our trekking through Marpha to Kagbeni and Muktinath then up to our final destination, Jomsom. We trekked the Annapurna Circuit, walking about twenty kilometers daily.

Going Back to Our Starting Point

We finished our trekking goal and began getting ready to go back to our start point and subsequently home. The schedule was to take a small plane back to Pokhara, and the next morning a second flight to Kathmandu, our initial meeting point.

We were at the airport on time for our 7:00 a.m. scheduled flight. However, the flight was cancelled due to extreme weather conditions. Since there was only one flight a day, we tried to get on the next day flight, but it was already full. There were two options left: fly by private helicopter or take the bus. Some decided to take the bus that was leaving soon. The rest (including me) hired a private helicopter to leave later that day.

Most of us gave our suitcases to the bus group to reduce the weight in the helicopter, keeping just a small backpack. The organizers fervently tried to get a helicopter to transport us to our next destination that day, but they didn't succeed. We searched all morning for some way to leave during the day, but it was impossible. Nothing worked. We were forced to stay one more night.

At the final stage of the trek, most of us, including me, had no Nepalese currency. There was only one ATM in town, but it was not working. Merchants only accept Nepalese-currency, no credit or debit cards. Therefore, I had no money or extra clothes, like most of us.

I asked someone to lend me money for dinner that night and breakfast the next morning; we all slept in our clothes. Fortunately, we found a teahouse with enough rooms for all of us.

Once at the teahouse, we contacted the other group to see if they had arrived at Pokhara, only to find out that they had gotten trapped due to a small accident, and all traffic was restrained. They had to spend the night on the road in the bus.

We could not believe what was happening. It was like, somehow, we were not supposed to leave the place at any cost. In my room, during meditation, I felt the need to open my heart. Inspired, I went to see a girl who had been ill during the day. I offered a Divine Mother healing session. She willingly agreed. I poured divine love onto her, feeling the connection with the Divine Feminine Force. When I finished her healing, I decided to wander through the upstairs part of the teahouse. In one room I found a lovely old lady bedridden. I tried to communicate with her, but the language barrier did not allow it. The next morning, with her daughter's permission, I spent some time with her and fed her oatmeal. Afterward, noticing that she was very pleased with my company, I spoke lovely words and prayers to her, invoking divine beings from all religions. When mentioning the names of Indian gurus, I saw tears in her eyes. This short time filled me with great peace and helped me to open my heart.

One hour later, we headed to the airport. The helicopter was on time and we left in groups of four. The view from the air was very dramatic as we weaved in and through a large gorge between the Annapurna and Dhaulagiri, two very impressive mountains. As we left, I filled the place with Love and Light in gratitude for all the opportunities I had received to grow.

From Pokhara, we flew to Kathmandu and stayed at the luxurious Hyatt Hotel for one night. The next morning, I went to the Kopan Monastery.

Recovering Codes in the Himalayas

I was told that in a powerful past life, I had left some codes at the Himalayas. My higher self-orchestrated this trip with the purpose to retrieve them in order to move forward in my spiritual path. However, days passed without my seeing anything familiar. On the seventh day of trekking, before falling asleep, I said out loud: *"Where are the codes? I can't wait to find them."* The next day, while walking the impressive Mustang district from Muktinath to Jomsom, I saw a spectacular oval-shaped stone that seemed perfectly cut in half. The stone contained strange figures and shapes. It was literally glittering under the sun's reflection in such a majestic and flawless way that I stared at it for a while. I was hypnotized by its beauty and perfection. Containing perfect symmetry, the codes were encrypted on it. It was impactful to see them with such clarity. I pleaded that they would be embedded in my consciousness, for without a camera, I could not capture their beauty.

Nepal Overview

Surprisingly, Nepalese cuisine was delicious! The Tibetan bread is a delicacy for me. Our guides and packers were the most inviting and warmest people ever. The tea houses were clean and comfortable, and the owners were expressions of kindness. These memoirs will live in my heart forever. I am grateful to all those who took part in it—the organizers, the group, the guides, and the packers exceeded my expectations.

The Kopan Monastery Visit in Kathmandu, Nepal

After finishing the Himalayan trekking, I decided to stay for a few days at Kopan Monastery in Kathmandu, which is a large Tibetan Buddhist monastery. The monastery provides courses and retreats in a picturesque hilltop setting, which is serene and peaceful. The views over the city below and the surrounding countryside mountains are spectacular. The monks and staff are very friendly and helpful. There are stupas, a library and gardens. My favorite part was a lonely terrace full of butterflies and chirping birds that invited solace and meditation. The rooms are plain yet comfortable. They observe a vegetarian diet. The sound bath offered by the monks at 5:30 a.m. is remarkable—you leave the temple renewed and stronger. The peace lasts throughout the day.

They offer meditations daily guided by a Buddhist nun named Thabten Wongmo. Her wisdom assisted me in reaching an unworldly state of consciousness about different themes. Here is one example of it.

One day, she marvelously explained how our attachment to an aversion can affect us. They create unnecessary pain. After her dissertation, she invited us to meditate on the following questions:
How many aversions do you have?
Have you been happier for holding them?
Are they giving you joy?
Have the persons involved changed due to your attachment to that aversion?

Looking at aversions from that perspective made me realize that I had been hurting myself by holding them. By changing that perception, I gained more autonomy and, therefore, peace.

Another day, she provided a speech about karma. Synthesizing, she said: *"If you want to know about your past lives, see your present life. If you want to see your future lives, check how you have been doing in this lifetime."* What a powerful teaching.

Thabten Wongmo resides in the monastery, and we became friends. She showed me around and assisted me during my time there. I asked her questions about being a nun, including about how hard it was to shave her head when entering the monastery. She answered, *"Not difficult at all."* When we said our farewells, she told me, *"I hope to see you again … with less hair."* I smiled and gave her a hug.

France Pilgrimage

"Nothing That Oppresses You Can Be Further from the Truth"

In our search for love and enlightenment, we may become easy prey for those with some kind of advantage, such as money, power, or the knowledge we believe we are looking for. In 2014, looking online for spiritual refuge, I found a group led by a blind lady. She claimed to channel Master Serapis

Bey. At that time, I did not have any experience and truly believed she was genuine. From the beginning, I acknowledged that she was feeding members' fears and illnesses, which was making them easier to control. Nevertheless, I joined a few events.

During a class held at her house when Master Yeshua's message came through me, she denied it was him and stated that no one could channel divine beings so quickly.

I participated in two more events, a cruise and a trip to France. During these events, she controlled the group through tantrums. One of the girls stepped out right after attending the cruise experience. Another lady had left the group abruptly, without any explanation. Which were probably signs that I began to notice. During the trip to France, she used abusive language because another lady and I failed to bring her personal belongings when she had ordered. It was an exhausting. Everything was in total disarray, including the organization. She decided that the five of us had to sleep in the car two nights because she did not like the places she or her assistant had reserved. We drove to the four corners of France in about seven days. It was an unpleasant experience. Due to the excessive time sitting in a car, I caught a cystitis infection that forced me to rest in my room for a few hours a day. I am deeply grateful that during this resting time I received the following life-changing warning:

> *"Sometimes things don't come from God.*
> *You are supposed to write—there is a lot to say.*
> *Yes, I come in the name of God, The Nameless One.*
> *You have been subdued;*
> *you have to look for the truth,*
> *the truth of your own God-Self.*
> *Move forward through your path.*
> *Nothing that oppresses you can be further from the truth."*

It was that type of message that makes you wake up from a nightmare. It injected in me the courage to break the chains. It urged me to recognize my own value and speak my truth. It is a tool that stimulates our path to liberation. Once back home, I left the group in love and gratitude for the experiences that in the long run assisted me to make better choices. I appreciate that she recommended a great book to me: *Dear and Glorious Physician* by Taylor Caldwell.

The Trail of Tears, North Carolina

When shopping for a cabin, Georgia was my first option. Since that was not possible, I focused on North Carolina. I fell in love with the very first cabin I saw. Curiously, it is situated in Cherokee County.

When a friend came to visit me, I took her for a horseback ride near my home. Once we started the trail, our guide announced that we were entering the Trail of Tears. *"What is that?"* I asked. This is what she said:

"In response to the Indian Removal Act, passed in 1830, more than 15,000 Cherokee Indians were forced from their homes in North Carolina and other states by the United States Army, beginning in May 1838. The 1,200-mile trek lasted six months. Along the way, an estimated 10 to 25 percent of the tribe died of disease, starvation and exhaustion."

I felt the energy of the place projecting a heavy density victim consciousness.

As we continued, we made a stop, and my friend found it easy to prompt her horse to gallop. When my horse intended to follow, I tried to stop it, which probably made the guide's horse nervous, because it kicked my horse twice. The first time I could handle it, but the second time my horse lost control. I tried to hold the reins—without success. In such a stressful moment, I heard the guide screaming: *"Be careful! Your horse is going backward, and there is a cliff behind you!"*

My experience with horses was very limited. I did know what to do except to cry out *"Archangel Michael, help me!"* As soon as I said that, my horse got cold feet and stopped. I looked backward to confirm that my horse was a few meters from the precipice. The guide came forth and punched my horse twice. Disheartened, I got off and walked back to the stables. In the midst of the confusion, something beautiful happened while we walked back. My horse (which was her personal horse) talked to me. He tried to put his head under my arm. He was very sorry for everything. That was the first time I sensed so clearly the feelings of a horse! What a blessing! I did not tip the guide because I was offended that she had punched the horse.

In the car, on our way back home, a reflection and a vision came to me: *"She did just like you did the other day when your cat bit you in the dark while you were sleeping, remember? You kicked the cat in response to a desperate intent to protect yourself. The guide was protecting you."* I had an image of me bringing her pink roses. Mother Mary talks to me through visions most of the time.

It took me a few days to put my judgments away and bring her two roses—one for my friend and one for me. She was ecstatic with gratitude. I repeated that later, and we became friends. She is a lovely human being.

Past Life in Cherokee Territory

Later on, during a session with a powerful healer, she saw a past life in which I was a member of the Cherokee tribe. I had been buried in the same territory where I was currently living. Aware of that, I decided to pay tribute to them. I rented a horse from my friend and dispersed rose petals along the Trail of Tears, filling the space with divine light and Christ Consciousness. It was a moment of joy and sadness at the same time. I felt reconnected to the sacredness of the place.

Days later, during meditation, a muscular, tall and handsome Indian male wearing a crown of white feathers showed up. He said: "Smile"
I asked: "*Who are you?*"
I heard: "*I am an aspect of yourself; I am smiling.*"
I could not believe it. It was a confirmation that I belonged to the tribe in the past. Still incredulous, I said: "*Do you belong to the Cherokee Tribe?*"
He: "*Yes, I was there at the Trail of Tears; that wasn't fun.*"
Me: "*I brought Christ Consciousness there.*"
He: "*Thanks for what you did.*"
Me: "*Thanks for guiding me. I love you.*"

As I continued in a trance state, I began speaking a strange language. I did not understand a word. In my ignorance, I said, "*Please speak English.*" Then I heard: "*There was a lot of pain there—pain and suffering that caused you to close your heart.*" I was astounded. It all made sense. I was part of the Cherokee tribe when they were forced to leave their homes. That event was very significant to me. That was the reason why I found the cabin exactly in the same geographic location in North Carolina. I had some unfinished business there.

Also, because electrical currents had been coming from my lower back up to my crown chakra, I asked if this was kundalini raising. I heard: "*The Kundalini needs to be raised.*" While I kept speaking more of what I assumed was the Cherokee language, I asked: "*How can I do it?*" I heard: "*Practice, practice, practice.*"

CHAPTER III
HEALING ABILITIES–A GIFT

"Focus on yourself.
Anything you do with love and gratitude will prevail.
Only the power of love triumphs in any situation.
Define what your truth is then stand on it.
Nobody can take you away from your truth.
Me: My truth is service to God above all.
How do I serve God?
Through service to humanity.
Me: How do I serve humanity?
By reaching them through God's messages."
"Of Me I Do Nothing. It's the God within Me Who Does It All."

My First Clients—Baby Chicken

My very first healing experience occurred when I was about six or seven years old. We had hens and chickens in the patio. When the little chickens died, a relative and I sat on the floor and placed them under a big, empty cans of crackers. Then we drummed it for a few minutes. That must have revived them, because they came back to life!

During my session with the Arcturians through Dr. Suzanne Lie, they reminded me of my healing abilities and mentioned the case of the chickens. At that moment, I had no idea what they meant. However, later on, I remembered it.

How did the chicken come back to life? Through sound? I would like to know.

The Empath in Me

I had no idea what being an empath was. I noticed that sudden feelings of sadness, stress and fear came to me out of nowhere. I was like a sponge, absorbing other people's feelings, pains and emotions without even realizing it. Here are a few events that caught me by surprise, but also assisted me in identifying myself as an empath.

One day, I suddenly began feeling very ill with nausea, headache, and general malaise that forced me to lie down and rest. After a while, all the symptoms mysteriously disappeared. Later that day, I learned that one of my sisters had been feeling so ill at the same time, that she required urgent medical attention.

On another occasion, I experienced deep sadness and emotional stress; later I learned that someone very close to me had gotten into a legal situation and had spent the night in a detention center.

Those two cases happened many miles away. Furthermore, a niece told me that in times of distress, she hears my voice and feels my presence. This is what she relayed:

While waiting at the bus stop one night, she suddenly felt weak and almost fainted. Still dizzy, she sat on the sidewalk to recuperate; at that moment, she heard my voice and felt a hand on her shoulder calming her down. She was scared but was able to board the bus without any help.

The second time, she was having an episode of depression and even contemplating taking her own life. She was weeping by the image of the Lady of Guadalupe when she heard my voice consoling her. She states that she immediately got up and felt uplifted. She's never had those thoughts again.

Another time, she called me to ask for assistance with a burning migraine episode. I began a Divine Mother Healing session. I noticed she was very quiet when I finished. I hung up presuming she had fallen asleep. The next day, she told me that during the session she went unconscious for a while and saw me in a white robe working on her with a man on each side. She mentioned that we were speaking in a strange tongue.

When she came back, the migraine was gone. What happened on those occasions? I would say that while our lower-self deals with the session, our higher-self travels dimensions where healing takes place.

First Healing Modalities I Practiced

Star Healing Intergalactic Energy and Divine Mother Healings

Early in 2014, Archangel Michael inspired me to receive training to practice Star Healing Intergalactic EnergyTM, which is taught by Kelly Hampton, an amazing channel and healer herself. The training took place in Mt. Shasta, California. I had the honor of practicing this modality on many people who benefited from it.

In 2016, I obtained certification as a Divine Mother Healer in a program facilitated by Connie Huebner online. It is a great healing style. I practice Divine Mother tools constantly. They have been my gateway to freedom.

Receiving Downloads to Practice My Own Healing Modality

One night in November 2018, Divine Yeshua came forth with the following message:

> *"I am Yeshua, I am Yeshua, I am Yeshua.*
> *The time has come for you to step into your truth,*
> *To step into your divinity.*
> *You are going to receive downloads and information*
> *That will help you to move forward into your path.*
> *Give more value to self-love."*

I certainly received more downloads and noticed that more healing modalities were coming into my awareness, along with an increase in my psychic abilities. It's like applying my divine self's wisdom. I am honored to be of service.

Light Coming from My Hands—I Am an Electric Conduit of Healing

In 2012, I noticed that in the dark, every time I touched my blanket sparks of light would show up. That had never happened before. I ignored them, but they kept appearing. In 2017, I had the honor of asking the amazing channel Julien Wells for his opinion on this, and this is how he responded:

"You are like a battery working. A battery has a positive and a negative side. You are basically emitting positive energy in your cells, in your body. You are more positively charged. You have a very alkaline body, which makes you a healer for people who have an acidic body. Most sickness comes from having a high level of acidity. You are a healer because you are a positive vibration, mentally and physically. You have electrons that are attracted to you and, when you touch someone or work with someone, you balance that energy. You balance the circuit with your abundance and their lack, because everyone wants to be in balance of positive and negative physical atoms—electrons. That is actually electricity on you and on your skin, like a light wire. There are even times when you can charge a watch on your wrist; you don't even need a battery, because your body produces electricity.

Technically, the heat that comes out of you generates electricity as a chemical process. But it also is just like the clouds. When you get hot and cold air, you get sparks of electricity that shift out. You are a battery, and people in need of healing are like depleted batteries. You can perform healings just by touching them or even just by being close to them. You are still drawing like positive electrons. You shift their bodies because you have a heat-generator mechanism within you. You have acidic and alkaline qualities in your body, and you have more alkaline production. Therefore, it generates energy, and this goes into the subtle energies of the aura."

His explanation gave me great confidence to embrace my healing abilities. I witness it when I cough in the dark and light comes from my throat. An episode of light happened during a lightning and thunderstorm. I was sleeping on the floor right in front of a window. When the light came through the window, a piece of blanket got attached to the right side of my face and it lit completely. It took me by surprise. I moved my sleeping bag away from the window, grateful that nothing had happened.

His enlightenment may support the following events.

A Neighbor Came for Lunch and was Healed

A nice neighbor I invited for lunch came in, saying: *"You told me you were a healer, right?"* I responded: *"Yes, sure."*

She added: *"I have had this elbow pain for a while. Can you heal it?"* As we were sitting down at the table, I smiled, for I heard a voice whispering in my ear: *"By the end of lunch, she will be healed."*

During lunch, I poured the divine love on her elbow. By the end, I asked her: "*How's your elbow doing?*" She started moving it and yelled: "*It does not hurt! Maybe just by the fact of being here with you it got healed!*" I came forth and held her elbow, giving it more love. That night, she sent me a few texts expressing her appreciation.

Six months later, she came into town and invited me for dinner. During dinner, she mentioned that her shoulder was hurting and that she could use some healing. I said, "*Yes, of course. Just come visit me.*" She never had the chance to do it, but since she'd asked, I sent healing energy. A few days later, she texted me to say: "*I think you are sending healing vibes my way, because it seems so much better! I don't know how you do that, but I am glad you do. That shoulder was giving me fits until I mentioned it to you. Now it's so much better, I can't even tell you!*"

I have to add that this type of healing is new for me. This was the first time I healed someone that way. Later, she texted: "*I never was a believer until I met you and have seen remarkable results.*"

Healing a Lady at Walmart (Murphy, NC)

While waiting at Walmart to change my car tires, I sat in the waiting room where there was another lady also waiting for her vehicle. She was staring at me, and I felt overdressed for fall. I said to her: "*Where I live, it is very cold.*" She asked where that was, and I said up on the mountains. She was in awe. Later, I started a conversation. When she got up to peek through the window at her car, I noticed a painful expression on her face. I asked her: "*Do your knees hurt?*" She looked at me with an affirmative expression. I said: "*Would you like me to help you?*" To my surprise, she nodded in agreement.

I asked her to relax while I placed my hands on her knees without touching them and poured love. She exclaimed: "*I can feel the heat coming from your hands!*" I kept doing my job. When I finished, I looked at her and she had tears in her eyes. I was touched by the purity of her heart. I recommended that she rest and drink a lot of water. She thanked me and I said goodbye, since my car was ready. I did not ask her name, but my heart was singing in joy and gratitude. Months later while writing this experience, I asked Mother Mary if this lady had been healed and I got a yes. The more I can help others, the happier I am.

An Interesting Approach I Discerned When Assisting Two People

Heal the Root of the Situation to Heal the Physical Pain

Many times, we run and hide from our emotions instead of using them to find the cause of the discomfort. This pattern locks the pain in the system, like locking it up in a closet and ignoring it whenever it cries: "*Let me out! I am hurting! Let me out!*" Then we use different things like the media, alcohol, food, sex, and so forth to numb it in order to avoid listening. This, in turn, complicates the matter and causes diseases or depression. I personally believe that each pain identifies with a trauma buried in our psyche.

By tracking the emotions intertwined with the pain, we take a huge step forward. The following are two interesting stories that may confirm this. In one case, the client was not ready to heal; in another, she willingly accepted her weakness and worked on it.

First story: This client developed a very bad infection in his body, which caused him a great deal of pain. He was forced to cancel his public presentations. I explained to him that the rash was a sign of an unresolved issue within. I detected that his present environment was toxic and not supporting his heart's desires. Gently, I provided information about self-love, self-compassion and courage to break with the old, and to trust the unknown. He recognized that as a truth but still refused to get out of his comfort zone to make changes. Consequently, the cycle continued. Months later, I had the chance to talk to him and witnessed that he was still in the same vicious circle. One can heal using medicines, but later another condition surfaces. His body was screaming for deep healing within.

To the contrary, the second client was willing to face her trauma and work on it, healing it completely as a result. According to her testimonial:

"*I humbly give the following testimonial to Lucero for the healings I have received from her. She is a remarkable healer who transcends love and beauty in all she meets. Her spiritual connection to the Divine is extremely evident in her presence and in her healings. My latest healing sessions with her were for a bout of vertigo I was experiencing. During the first session, my dizziness was so prevalent that I couldn't lift my head from the bed without the room spinning so much that it caused me to vomit. Lucero did a phone session that day as I lay in bed. Although the vertigo continued, I was much improved by the next day—no more vomiting, and the dizziness was at a much lower intensity. The next session that I had, Lucero received information from the Divine that I needed to work on my inner child. She gave me examples of how to do this work, and I'm in the process of following her suggestions. I'm happy to say that my vertigo symptoms are almost completely gone and I'm continuing to work on my inner child—she needs a lot of love, and Lucero saw that!*

Lucero is truly divinely guided. Her work infuses love into the overall physical, emotional, spiritual and multi-dimensional being, allowing the healing to take place always for the client's highest good. Lucero's intentions emanate pure, unconditional, authentic love, and her gifts are great. Thank you for sharing your gifts with me Lucero, for I am forever grateful."
—P.G. Poughkeepsie, NY

Lesson I Learned

Thanks to these two wonderful people, I was able to empirically prove my theory that negative emotions are just symptoms and that by tracking them we can find the root of it. Each one worked in a perfect way to provide what I needed at the moment.

My Favorite Technique

Using the power of love, I may clear a person's energy field of any imbalances or disturbing energies that are either causing pain or circumventing the normal flow of life force in their systems. This can be done in person or remotely. I applied the energy of Love on my neighbor and on the lady at Walmart.

> *"Just be you.*
> *I said: How?*
> *Allow yourself to be you.*
> *Self-acceptance, self-love, patience.*
> *Just be you,*
> *I am Divine Mother, I come in the name of God,*
> *I come in the name of truth,*
> *I want you to let go of the past."*

Some Testimonials

"My experience with the Star Healing Intergalactic Energy has been marvelous. I always wished to find a treatment that would heal my constant back pain. I have had several surgeries over the years. When one was done on my spinal cord, the doctor's recommendation was that I wear a corset to support my back day and night. This device was restrictive and extremely uncomfortable. My personal life was miserable. I was praying for a solution. Fortunately, I had a session with Lucero, and the pain left almost immediately! Pain is gone, and I don't need to use that annoying device anymore. My headaches disappeared as well. Besides that, my addiction to sugar and chocolate has vanished. Now I can work around the house and sleep much better. I feel great! Thank you."
—L. R. Boca Raton, FL.

"Before the session, I was feeling sad and depressed about some situations in my family. After the session, I experienced a great sense of peace and relaxation. Depression and sadness are gone. Thank you very much for your help. I am sure you will have a big success, for you are a wonderful being with a great heart that helps without conditions. Just talking to you makes me feel more confident."
—Ivan. Coral Springs, FL.

"I want to thank you for helping me. Before the session, I had constant back pain in the lower back. I have had three surgeries in the last thirty years. My symptoms were pain and weakness. Ten days after the session, the pain and weakness in the lower back had disappeared completely! Four months have passed, and I am pain free! My back feels great. I will be grateful forever for your freeing me of that problem in my life. God bless you."
—D. P. Hollywood. FL.

CHAPTER IV
MY LIBERATION

"I am the heart of Sananda.
Open your heart's door.
Let the golden light come out.
Expand it to your surroundings,
then to planet Earth.
Send it to all around you, good or bad.
Send it to every person you have had physical contact with in this lifetime
or another lifetime.
The shaking of your right hand was indicating that you have to write.
I want you to write the sound of the rain."

The Deepest Part of The River

Such a display of affection and encouragement from the Highest Realms of Light assisted me to move forward. I used to believe that as humans we were small, insignificant and limited. I thought that God never talked to anybody and that He was far away, moving strings and providing pain or joy according to one's behavior or, worse, his caprice! A big discovery for me was to learn that God sustains both aspects, feminine and masculine. Such a truth made a lot of sense and injected my soul with great hope and deep trust.

My story is the story of every being's pilgrimage through despair and life-darkness. Living in survival mode most of my life, it was hard to see the beauty of my soul in its total grandeur. The most difficult part of this writing has been to expose the dark part of my existence. It took me a while to see the importance of sharing these stories. The last time I protested, I heard:

"*There is a higher purpose in sharing them. They represent a great advancement of everybody's spiritual development.*"

"*Why?*" I asked.

I heard, "*Because the world is based on pain and suffering, and others may identify with your story.*"

Me: "*But I may hurt others by exposing their lies.*"

Voice: "*That may help them to face themselves as well. And others may recognize those patterns in their lives and take measures to heal them.*"

Me: "*So here I am. Help me, God.*"

Growing Up in Colombia

My mother was three months pregnant with me when her eight-year-old son died in an accident. In her despair, she locked herself up and refused to eat for a long time. Unbeknownst to her, I was in her womb. It was an intense and deep trauma for both of us. Apparently, her grief lasted way after I was born. She was not able to even acknowledge me at birth. It took her a while to accept me. I suffered with her too. As an adult, comprehending that my inner baby was wounded was not pleasurable.

My father passed away when I was six years old, leaving my mom with four children and without any source of income. His inclination to alcoholism caused us to lose everything we had before his departure. A few days after he passed, the landlord came drunk to our place in the middle of the night and broke the windows, demanding rent money. The worst aspect of this situation was not just the lack of food or the scarcity that we faced daily but the low state of consciousness my mom fell into that affected me. I began feeling guilty for being there, guilty for eating any food we had, guilty for not being able to help my family.

I used to wait for the light to be turned off at night to cry and ask God to give me all the pain and suffering they were going through, for I did not want to see them suffering. There were times when we did not have anything to eat after school or before bed. In fourth grade, my mom took me to spend a school year with some family members who lived in a small town. I remember going there with holes in my shoes. A great day was when my teacher, Sister Maria Gladys, took me inside the convent and opened a box with new shoes for me! I will never forget the smell of a new pair of leather shoes. That was the best year of all.

My mother's suffering throughout her life made her angry and bitter. She projected a great sense of fear, resentment, and hatred toward life on everyone around her. Growing up was almost a torture due to her extreme controlling and negative behavior.

Our relationship was always on the rocks. Living in peace with her rules was hard. She used to predict or curse everything she did not like. Even though I was attending law school in the mornings and working at a drugstore in the evenings, I never had the freedom of going to the movies or a party without her.

I was eighteen years old when I met my first husband. We began dating, but the first time I came home at 10:00 p.m., she was waiting for me behind the door. As soon as I entered, she hit me with a belt.

Months later, I decided to break her rules and take a weekend vacation. When she searched my backpack and found my boyfriend's shirt in it, she cut it into pieces, full of anger. She said she could not live with a whore and threw me out of the house. That caused me financial hardship, for my part time job did not provide enough income to support myself.

Healing Archetypal Patterns Together

Many years passed. Only in 2017 did I begin to notice my mother's darkness. A mother is a symbol of love and dedication; however, in my case, that symbol is missing. I always detected that she was a very resentful person who never had any happiness no matter how much love and attention I gave her. It was a harrowing moment when I found out the truth.

Everything unfolded in a perfect way. My psychic abilities have been increasing since my awakening. The truth comes to me in the form of visions. That is how I saw that a powerful evil entity had taken control of her. This control has been happening for many lifetimes, and both of us have come together in many of them. The reason is that we have to heal that pattern. This is the story.

Becoming Aware of Her Dark Side

I have read that we all have a dark side. In my case, it took me 55 years to uncover my mother's. It was impossible to ignore it. Besides her harshly critical and demeaning attitude, every time she visited me, I became ill and my work projects got ruined. The flowers and plants wilted without a reason.

The last time she left my place, I began feeling weak. I felt like I was losing my life force; I was crying and feeling depleted. It was like a big dark cloud hovering over me, disrupting everything including my sleep patterns.

One night I woke up in the wee hours to clearly see dark energy coming from a painting I had on the wall above my bed. My ordeal had just started. I was under constant psychic attacks. All my business plans and invitations to talk about my healings fell apart.

I fell into a deep state of desolation. My bed, my blankets, my desk, all went to the dumpster. I could not concentrate. Nothing gratifying could go through. It was like the whole place was against me. I realized she had brought a very dark magic. When I asked her for an explanation, she responded in a very cold way: "*It is not my fault that your plants died, and you get sick when I am there. I have nothing to do with that.*" I was inconsolable. Basically, I had to get rid of everything. All my belongings ended up in the dumpster, and I slept on the floor. Then everything began to make sense. That bad energy had been sabotaging my existence.

The biggest disappointment of all was to find out that my ex-husband and my mom joined forces to make me come back to him through dark magic. He gave her money to carry out that venture. I have never confronted them about that. I have been healing silently, but now it's time to speak.

Opening My Heart to Compassion

I finally had the courage to set boundaries, not just with my mother, but with all those who were seeking to control me. I have not seen her for two years. Even though I kept feeling her negativity in my energy field, I found a way to manage the attacks by sending divine love. However, in October 2019, I felt she was moving her cords again. A nasty presence tried to penetrate my mind. This time I realized I had to do something extraordinary to put an end to it. Thus, facing my fears, I called her. I used a neutral place like a park or parking lot to talk to her so that I would feel safer.

As soon as she answered the phone, I asked her to listen carefully to what I needed to tell her. I let my heart talk. I said: "*I love you, I bless you, I forgive you, and I release you.*" She said she loved and forgave me too. Then, I said: "*Mom, I know that a dark entity, an evil spirit has been controlling you.*" She went speechless.

"*An entity has ruined your life. But you are powerful and strong enough to let it go.*" To my surprise, she answered: "*I don't know how; I tell them to go, but they come back.*" I said: "*Tell them to go into the light! You can do it; you still have time to stop this control. You can do it.*" I was stunned. We had never approached this issue before. Then we said good-bye and I hung up. It was a meaningful conversation. I went home and cried.

The next day, I felt her energy again in the kitchen. Nonetheless, this time was different. Looking for advice, I entered into a meditative state. On this occasion, she was looking for help. I asked her what she wanted, and she answered: "*To be loved and recognized.*"

My heart opened immediately. My greatest desire had been to guide her to the light and express only love and tenderness toward her. I asked: "*How can I help her?*" A vision came forth: A beautiful star in her heart and another in her forehead. I asked her higher-self permission to activate them with the love and the light of Divine Mother. She needed assistance, so the angels came to help, too. Now, after two years of drama, we are able to work on her behalf. It is a glorious moment not just for me but for the world, because this pattern has been debilitating humanity for eons.

I am sure the light shone through her. I really love and miss her. I also visualized the evil entity in my hand, and I put it in my heart. I know my heart is strong and can handle it. Wish me luck, I am just an apprentice.

Reflection

I have seen the same pattern in many families. It is so treacherous that it goes unnoticed until someone or an event brings light on it. A bad energy can take control to keep families separated and in despair. It is time to do something about it.

Only through love and compassion can we vanquish this dark magic and manipulation. I am not asking anybody to put up with any abuse whatsoever. I myself set boundaries with her and others, as I narrate further. Nonetheless, I hold them in the light and the love of the Creator. Because if we get angry, we reinforce it.

Another Truth Came Afloat During A Psychic Healing Session- Child Molestation

One night in 2005, I woke up in the middle of the night sweating and my heart beating as fast as ever. When I sat in bed I clearly heard: "*You have not forgiven your father.*" Concerned about it, I began thinking about the reasons I would need to forgive him. The only one that came across was the fact that he left us without any financial means to survive due to his alcoholism. I found the issue futile but, even so, I forgave him.

My father passed away when I was about six years old. The only memory I have of him is he taking me by the hand very early in the morning. I don't remember anything about his face, his actions, nothing. But I remember missing him as a provider when we suffered financial scarcity after his death.

Now, in 2019 another truth is about to be discovered. Lately, I have been having nightmares with sexual content whenever I slept past 5 a.m. The image of Jon Benet Ramsey has been appearing to me since 2008. After this session, she came forth again. I am not sure if she has a message for me or just wants me to check her story. Also, when working on raising the energy of life, known as Kundalini, I sensed that there was something stuck in the base of my spine or root chakra. Then, more signs kept coming and, finally, the truth shone through a psychic session I had scheduled weeks before. When I was asked for my intention, I abruptly said: "*Was I molested when little?*" It came out like something I had been waiting to say out loud, even though I was not conscious about it.

What the healer said sounded like a horror movie. I missed the moment when after watching a horrific show I could comfort myself saying: "*Oh, it is just a movie, a fantasy.*" This time I couldn't do that. It was my own terrifying film.

My father molested me and my sisters. And, in the session, the image of a priest also came forth. The healer saw him taking me by the hand. But, not to buy fresh warm bread like my mom used to tell me when growing up. He was taking me to a Catholic priest who took advantage of my innocence, as he did. He made deals with the priest, probably to "save him from hell."

All emotions came pouring out, disappointment, sadness, frustration, betrayal to mention just a few. I cried a lot, walked in the rain, cried again. It is an excruciating truth from which I can't escape and can't change. I pray to

God to assist me in keeping my mind in control of negative thoughts about this fact, to take ownership of the story, face it and heal it.

I understand that the most powerful weapons I have are unconditional love, compassion and forgiveness. In order to finish the vicious circle and liberate ourselves and, very likely, assist them to move forward. There is only way to get there, by opening the heart. There are no shortcuts, it is simple and direct. Only the heart may heal our wounds.

I began observing the facts from a higher perspective, realizing that these people were so lost in their addictions and traumas that they deserve compassion. Not pity, for that opens the door to tolerance. We cannot tolerate abuse of any kind from anybody.

I understand that staying in victim consciousness would only amplify the negative forces, impeding me to advance. So, I began my own campaign. In meditation, I say out loud: *"I love you, I bless you, I forgive you and, I release you."* This practice creates a spread of elevated emotions that forms a protective web around me.

This story reflects the pain from sexual abuse which millions worldwide have suffered and are experiencing. This is why I was guided to expose it. Train your mind, make it understand that the heart is in control. The mind can't forgive. ONLY THROUGH AN OPEN HEART and meditation to calm the mental body we can accomplish true and complete forgiveness and healing.

I would like to lovingly suggest to my brothers and sisters who are attracted to alcoholic beverages to control their intake; for alcohol itself as well as cigarettes and drugs attract entities that may lead humans to do things that they will never do in a sober state of mind and that may regret later. We deserve freedom from any and all external influences.

My father got addicted to alcohol which might have led him to do things that were in discordance with his soul purpose.

First Marriage Experience

At age eighteen, after my mom threw me out of the house, I moved in with my boyfriend. I was going through the 3rd semester of law school. Besides the two amazing children we had, life with him was torture. These are some of the events that took place.

He got trapped in alcohol and other vices. Hostility and aggression were in control. Weekends were full of horror. After partying for days, he used to come home in the middle of the night to play music so loudly that nobody could sleep. He would wake up the children and force me to listen to his complaints until the morning hours. On different occasions, my children and I had to run out of the house in our nightgowns in the middle of the night, so afraid of his threats of burning the house down. He would break windows and scream at everybody.

One time during a fight, the ring I was wearing broke the skin above my right eyebrow, causing it to bleed. He took me to a hospital, where I got some stitches. I felt embarrassed, abused, and lonely. From my perspective, my life was a disgrace. I was nothing. I had no self-esteem.

I cannot count the times I left the house with the children. At first, I asked my sisters to give us a room while I was looking for a job. In doing so, I missed a great number of law school classes. He always went looking for us, asking for another chance. I fell into that trap many times.

In Colombia, it is very hard to support a family alone without an education, so I decided to work hard to finish law school. It was not easy at all, but nothing could stop me. As soon as I graduated, I divorced him. I moved away with the children to another city and state. However, he found us and came asking for another opportunity. I refused to go back. However, he was able to convince our six-year-old son to go back with him. My heart was broken. I did not have peace anymore without my son. A few months later, I went back. He tried to stay sober for a while, but later, the violence resumed.

One night he came home drunk and forced me to listen to his insults. Threatening me with matches, he set my hair and pajamas on fire. That was the last act of violence. I left him for good. When I told my mother about this disturbing event, her advice was: "*You have to stay. Don't leave the house.*" I was heartbroken by her lack of support.

His inclination to alcohol and other things opened the doors to the dark forces. He became a spiritual terrorist, destroying everything around him.

Years later, I immigrated to the United States with just my daughter, for he did not allow my son to leave the country. Finally, two years later, my son moved in with us. It was a joyful day.

An Event that Opened the Door to Forgiveness

One night while living in Florida, I was studying with my door closed. Suddenly, I saw the image of my estranged first husband knocking on my door, with a great deal of pain and anguish on his face. This had never happened to me before. In my nervousness, the only thing I could do was to get on my knees and pray for him. Days later, I found out that, at the same time I had this vision, he had undergone a terrible automobile accident that almost took his life, miles away in Colombia. I understood that when we are in a situation of danger, our soul goes out looking for help. I am honored to be of service. Curiously, I had just read the book *Messages from the Masters* by Bryan Weiss—a wonderful volume that opened my eyes to understand that life goes beyond life. This experience opened my heart to compassion toward him. I was not angry anymore.

Second Husband Trapped in the Astral Level

The Arcturians' Assistance

Once in the United States, I wed for the second time. Life together was acceptable; however, after a few years, he began getting enraged over the smallest details. One night, he told me to leave his house. He later regretted it and asked me to stay. However, after living such a horror-filled life in Colombia with my first husband, I did not want to take a chance. I moved out with my children.

The separation was not the main point. The nightmare began years later when he passed. His astral presence haunted me everywhere. My life became a war in which I could not see what I was fighting against. Day and night, I was harassed by whatever had taken possession of him. I had no joy anymore. My business declined; friends stopped talking to me for no reason. My checking account got hacked. My children's lives changed as well. My memory declined and health problems surfaced. It was like he was on a mission to constantly sabotage my life.

One day, I opened the medicine cabinet, and a garden snake was right on top of my little make-up bag. It seemed like someone had just put it in there. The interesting thing is that the cabinet was tightly closed. There was no way a snake could had sneaked in there. From where did it come? It took me a while to recover from it.

One evening, I was working from home when I saw his figure at the door. I was petrified. I did not tell anybody. Then he showed up a second time. I realized that he was somehow caught in a lower vibration. I needed some expert help. Somebody recommended a medium, and I made an appointment. According to her, he appeared with a hand in his heart, asking for forgiveness. Back home, I looked online and found *Radical Forgiveness* by Colin Tipping. Hoping to finish this nightmare, I bought it and went through the whole process. But even though the process is excellent, the trial continued. It actually got worse.

I could not sleep, day or night. Sleep deprivation deteriorated my normal life in an alarming way. I was haunted and persecuted non-stop. His presence was chasing me everywhere. Even in public places I was afraid to go to the bathroom. Deep inside, I knew it was a personal war.

I tried to get help from the Catholic Church, but their minds are so limited, they denied everything. That was a bad choice. I found Dr. Susan Shumsky's books. They helped me understand about lost souls, and I would say that my reconnection with God started at a prayer level, for I kept thinking that He was a judge who determines who deserves this and who does not.

I had been indoctrinated to worship an angry, punishing, fake god. How wrong that is!

Those who believe in that should reconcile with the real, loving, and tender God. How? Connecting with the power of your heart. Throughout this book, I am giving you the tools to accomplish it.

I was far from remembering that we have the power to create our own destiny, and that I had chosen those experiences to heal not just my own wounds but the wounds of others, as well.

Divine Assistance Came Forth—The Arcturians

Finally, after five years of struggle, I came across Dr. Suzanne Lie's website. She is a psychotherapist who has established communication with the Arcturians, celestial beings from the Arcturus galaxy—the brightest star in the Bootes constellation. They manifest only unconditional love, and their sole intent is to assist our planet in ascending into a higher dimension. This was the help I had been looking for!

They explained that because my ex-husband had died in a very low state of consciousness, he became an easy target for the dark forces. He was looking for help, but my fear had made things worse. They gave me information about my life mission and childhood traumas, and then showed him a way to freedom. They basically transmuted anger into unconditional love and forgiveness to heal this issue. What a relief! The light shone through.

The biggest lesson was to acknowledge how important it is to hold a positive outlook while in physical form. He was a wonderful man, but his unhappiness made him more vulnerable. This event was really a blessing that propelled me to learn more about paranormal experiences, reincarnation, karma, and, more importantly, how to assist lost souls to find their way to freedom. On top of that, it opened my heart to Divine Source in gratitude.

In 2014, in one of my meditations in the wee hours, Mahavatar Babaji came forth with this precious advice:

> *"I want you to get out of your prison.*
> *I want you to fly.*
> *Love your brother as yourself.*
> *Fill every situation with love,*
> *even those that do not please you.*
> *Joy is the key.*
> *Smile to obtain joy.*
> *I am joy."*
> BABAJI

Third Husband, Another Nightmare

In 2005 when I met my third husband, I was mesmerized by his intelligence and charm. I thought he was everything I had wished for. It was a lot of fun at the beginning, but his surreptitious controlling and manipulative behavior gradually began to unravel.

Signs I Ignored

One night after I moved in with him, I woke up with his face on top of mine, repeating: *"And you cannot even function without me."* It scared me, but I did not think it was relevant. Another day, he said in anger: *"I will cut your wings."* The relationship reached a point where I was afraid of leaving the house at night without him, afraid that I would not be able to answer the phone when he called me. I was afraid to disagree with any of his decisions, for he was the one who must have the last word on everything, from the living room curtains to my hairstyle. He planned our vacations to strategically align with his needs.

I Became an Object

I constantly felt trapped in deep waters, in a state of fear and unable to escape. Afraid to make him angry, I muted myself. Again, I was in a miserable relationship, just under a different layout. I felt lonely most of the time, for he was hardly present. His body could have been there, but his soul was somewhere else. He was usually busy following his "all-day gambling" and complaining that he did not have enough money or time. This made me feel guilty for any extra expenditures. I guess that was his intention.

I was under the illusion that I had to put up with everything he did in order to help him change. I had lost the real concept of love. This type of individual is very incisive and will eventually make you feel responsible for his misery. He threatened me in a very subtle way that he might die if I left him.

My Awakening

Divine Mother classes enhanced my connection with the Divine. My true self came out of hiding. The higher I went, the wider the gap between us became. We were living in different dimensions. Once the masks are off, life may become heavy and complicated for all parties involved.

I began to see the truth in every aspect of my life. I saw myself interwoven by invisible ties, clouding my mind. The more I advanced in my spiritual development, the more truth kept emerging. It was like a movie—a scary one. The process of uncovering the deceit was not sweet. It was agonizing, actually. My soul was hungry for love, but not the human love that causes pain and confusion. I was desperate to find the divine love that brings rapture and bliss. The magnificent support from the Divine Realm rapidly heightened my spiritual development. I observed that the current belief system on which I based my lifestyle was in discordance with my Inner Self.

Separation Process—Leaving the House

Hopeless and disappointed, I decided to step out of my comfort zone and cut ties with everything I had built so far. After a huge, invisible battle, I made the valiant decision to leave everything behind. This time, my reconnection with the Divine Source, God, came to assist us through the whole process with great love and compassion, even though my husband was not conscious of it at all.

Here are some dialogues I found in my journal written during the process:

"*Beloved God, why I do I feel like this? How? Without a place to go. I feel like I am in the wrong place with the wrong people—like in a prison. I feel I cannot get out of this torture. Why can't I find the balance? Is it my soul's desire to spend the rest of my years with him? To experience duality? I don't want to experience duality anymore. I want to live in the fifth dimension experiencing only unconditional love. But how can I do it living with him? I cannot, that is for sure. Should I leave? If so, where should I go?*"

Voice: "*If I tell you to get out of this place, what would you do? Would you actually get out? Or would you just keep wondering if it is the right thing to do?*"

Me: "*I have been denying the truth. The truth is that it is impossible to stay in the frequency of love and peace around him. I am not listening, yes, that is right. Why can't I leave him?*"

Voice: "*Because you need more trust. TRUST his infinite self. TRUST.*"

Me: "*Why don't I want to leave? Because I am afraid. Afraid of what?*"

Voice: "*Afraid that he will not be able to live without you.*"

Me: "*I cannot believe I am afraid, afraid of his anger, afraid of his hatred, afraid of his darkness. Do I need more courage?*"

Voice: "*You tell me.*"

Me: "*Suppose I take my suitcase with my clothes, where should I go? Where would I go to serve God?*"

Voice: "*Let's go back to that part where you are afraid of his hatred, his darkness, and his anger. If you live another's agenda, you are not honoring yourself.*"

One day I wrote:

"*Beloved Creator,*

I feel like I'm in a prison. Why is it so difficult to leave this place? Is it because of the money thing? Or is it because you want me to display my courage? I did it in front of the therapist and felt so good. I even got a rainbow from Mother Nature. How about if I just get a suitcase and put my clothes in there and leave? Where should I go? I am still so confused about that! Should I stay here for a while more to see what happens?"

August 2015 - A Pink Cloud Talked to Me

"Yesterday morning, I felt the urge to go outside of the house, and I saw this beautiful pink cloud with a gorgeous gold color on the right side. I wondered why it had color, since the sun was not out yet. It was like the rainbow that came right in front of me without any rain, sun, or anything. It was just there. Amazingly, the gold cloud talked to me and gave me the best advice ever, advice that changed my life. I heard the words "divide assets." I went back inside and told him to divide the assets before divorcing, and he loved the idea. That gave us peace of mind during the storm. Thank you!"

August 29, 2015

"Finally, I decided to leave on September 9. My God, my fortress in whom I trust, I have twenty days left here. I am doing my best to stay calm, but every day is more difficult. He comes home with different personalities. He hurts me with his way of talking, pointing his finger at me. His wish is to keep me tied up. The faster I leave, the better it will be. The tension around the house could be cut with a knife."

September 1, 2015

"We signed the marital division of assets. I accepted what he proposed. It is not my intention to fight. I just want inner peace. I decided to move to Sedona, Arizona."

I wrote in my journal: "Dear God, today I practiced what the book Conversations with God says: 'What you resist, persists.' Very true. I had refused to face him, and every day was getting harder. I could not even look at him; it made me angry to see his loser attitude. Finally, today we spent time together, and I exploded. It was like a mix of emotions. I cannot deny I love him and that it is painful to leave him. I feel like I am leaving a child behind. At least I felt better energy coming from him. I looked at him today with unconditional love and was able to tell him that I loved him. These last twenty days together, I will try to be the best possible so he can let me go in peace. Thank you, beloved Mother-Father God, for your guidance."

Unbeknownst to me, the separation would show his real face.

His Harassment in Sedona, Arizona

I moved far away, hoping to regain some tranquility. Nonetheless, that was just the beginning of the next ordeal. His real self was uncovered. It was shocking to learn about his psychic abilities and to find out that he manages to do astral travel to keep controlling, watching, and harassing me even miles away.

It reached a point of insanity. I felt under pressure day and night. I know now why, during our marriage, I always sensed his presence, even after he had left the house. Horrible, isn't it? Besides that, every time I shared with him something that had happened in my family, it was like he knew it and had the answer ready. Many things started to make sense. It was like opening a can of lies. My little granddaughter said more than once: "He is sitting by my side, telling me to ask you questions." On one occasion, sensing not just his presence but also more entities that came with him, I called upon Jesus Christ and Buddha to help me and take them out of my space. When they took him, I heard his screaming voice repeating: "This is not fair." It was appalling.

Later, I had the blessing to find a solution to stop this drama. Keep reading.

I Filled My Third Ex-husband's Heart with Divine Light

A Celestial Solution

Archangel Michael recommends filling a person's heart with Divine Light to ameliorate any density. I lovingly filled my ex-husband's heart with divine light and love for three weeks, three times a day. After that period of time, my phone rang. It was him. He was much calmer, and we could handle a conversation.

Two years later, I sensed his negativity invading my space again. I made an attempt to alert him about the harm he caused in doing so, but he ignored me. It is important to acknowledge that damaging emotions such as anger create an equally charge of negative energy that surrounds all those involved increasing confusion and pain. I keep praying for him daily, filling his heart with Divine Love.

Another Case with Similar Energy

It seems like this was a discovery period for me. This is a story about a lady I met in Colombia when she was eight years old and I was eighteen. Our relationship was not optimal. I always felt a very high negativity about her, but I blamed it on her young age. Years passed, and we each moved to different countries. When I began doing healings, I offered her my services. One time, while on the phone, she told me that she was very depressed and sad.

I immediately offered a free spiritual retreat at my place. Even though she had to travel far, she grabbed the opportunity. At the end of the retreat, she seemed very pleased with the results. The day she was leaving my place, I noticed a strange attitude about her, like she needed to say something but didn't do it. Once I returned from the airport, I sensed many little men without feet following me around my house, checking over my shoulders and controlling everything I did. It was traumatic because none of my methods worked to get them out of my space. I was in a constant battle, deprived of sleep, putting up with those things until I found a new method that worked. It is listed in Chapter III as "the vacuum."

I did not connect the fact that my friend might have left them in a conscious way. Therefore, I continued assisting her with more sessions until the truth came forth. She is a carrier of something similar to what my mom has, "a heartless witch."

Everything made sense. While providing her with Divine Mother Healing sessions, I reached a deep façade that seemed like a strong wall I could not dissolve. I advised her of that situation with great honesty, but she basically did not care. The next time I tried to help her, the truth showed up. I saw the same evil entity that appeared in my mom's field attached to her. I went paralyzed in horror. However, trusting that she would show some reaction and a desire to heal that pattern, I told her. I channeled a message that came through, advising her that this entity had been harming her children and all those around her. She denied it and blamed her boyfriend's ex-wife. I said no, it had been with you for a very long time. She denied it again. I rather stepped away from her life.

Nonetheless, the visions kept coming. I saw clearly that she had been entering my space all these years, watching me. And she kept doing it. The difference was that now I noticed it. It became so annoying that I sent her an email asking to stop entering my space. Her only answer was an *"OK."* I began analyzing our relationship. I lived near her for twelve years. She was mean as a child; I could see how she enjoyed seeing others fighting.

The truth always shows up. Recreating my relationship with her, I realized that every time I was far from home, she would text me and ask where I was. I had no idea that she also travels in an etheric form to control others.

After I'd become aware of her behavior, she texted me one day while I was away from home. I deleted it, ignoring her. As soon as I did, I felt her rage and many negative entities surrounding me. I put myself together and asked them if she had sent them. The answer was "yes." I call upon Archangel Michael to show them the way to the light. It was stressful to confirm that someone you trusted was in reality an enemy.

Something I learned about these types of people is that they hardly smile or laugh spontaneously; nothing makes them happy, for their hearts are compromised. Perceive them with compassion and without judgment but set boundaries.

The Last One

Around 2012, I found a man online who claimed to perform divine healings. He was supported by another healer whom I trusted blindly at that time. Enthusiastic about it, I hired him to do healings on me and others, and I referred him to friends. The initial reports were accurate, and I believed in him without a doubt.

Later on, I noticed that the reports were not as accurate as they had been at the beginning and, personally, I did not see any changes. I started using his services less and less. Then, in 2018, I saw him on a social media platform, and we became friends. Meanwhile, he told me he would be near my area and mentioned his desire to meet me. I had not proved anything against him, so I agreed.

Some eerie events took place before and after I met him. Strangely, my dental bridge fell off. I did not think much of it and went to the dentist to repair it.

The next day, a funny smell appeared by the septic tank. The technician came to confirm that the pump that was supposed to last twelve years was broken.

This "healer" invited me for dinner, during which he warned me that negative beings were harassing him and that they may come after me, too. The second day, we intended to go trekking, but at the start of the trail my stomach got bloated and my body itched so much that I went back home.

I began feeling uneasy about it. I entered into meditation. I received that his intentions were less than benevolent and confirmed that his healings were suspicious. In other words, the first healing may work; however, discordant entities come back days later to harass the client, so they have to keep using his services.

I started to put it all together. I was struck by the fact that he proclaimed doing the same activities with his grandson that I had done with my granddaughter—the same movies, the same way to make popcorn, the same activities. How did he know those facts? In a few words, he had been watching and controlling me without my knowledge. I connected the dots and realized I had been listening to a voice that had been telling me what to do next, but the voice sounded so familiar, I ended up listening to it.

The two times I saw him in person were enough to see the truth. The story repeated again. He had been intruding into my space. He tried to keep doing it, only this time I was aware of it and told him to stop. I would like to add that when I wrote and then burnt a forgiveness letter to him, the harassment stopped. The process of forgiveness is very powerful. No matter what system we may use, it makes a great difference in our lives and the lives of those we forgive.

It is important to take action, for these individuals can control our lives and ruin anything they want if we don't detect it on time to stop them.

The Final Piece of the Puzzle

In February 2019, the discomfort in the back of my heart guided me to request a session with a powerful healer. She discovered the root of my ordeals.

It is important to share that as soon as she mentioned the name of the entity, a great, huge light came from above, totally covering me. At that moment, I lost consciousness. I must have entered into a deep trance state, because I don't remember anything that happened afterward. At the end, I was so exhausted, I just wanted to rest and forget about it. Yet, three months later, while writing this book, the pain came back. I was guided to listen to the recording. It made me understand that I had to share it with you.

I must say that this truth has not been easy to understand or get used to. Only through the power and love of God can I find solace. I trust my Divine Self and the power within to give me the certainty that ALL is and shall be forever WELL.

Here is a portion of what she channeled:

"First of all, the energy configuration of consciousness has shifted from what it was in the years of the apocalypticism to now because we crossed the threshold of Light, and those who are ready in their hearts and had said yes to the highest potential of their consciousness have been supported and accelerated in many ways.

Your energy for the Divine Mother is powerful for the awakening of the Feminine God Force on the planet, because you are an anointed messenger of the Divine Mother. But *there is an archetypal force that has tried to destroy you. When I looked into your field, I saw that you had struggled to protect yourself and those who you loved.*

You have never been able to completely resolve and release the patterns of energy that are caused by the force that this negative energy is coming with. It is not your imagination; you have been attacked, and constantly. If I am wrong, please tell me, but I heard the FIRST OF ALL affirming that you are an anointed messenger of the Divine Mother, and that you have a power that has agreed to awaken the light for yourself and for the Earth. And there is yet a higher potential for your work as a messenger and a medium of the Divine Feminine Force on this planet. You have not reached the full power of who you are and why you incarnated.

It is not because of the resistance. It is because of the evolution of your consciousness that you have to go through situations that are like initiations for your life choices. I get very, very lightheaded as I channel this, very lightheaded. You are in the process.

The directives of the High Council of Light have supported and assisted you through this acceleration of ascension and awakening of the total of your being. So, you have lots of energetic support. The purpose of this channeling is to affirm and empower your God-given gifts and to know that, if this entity could have taken you over, it would have, and it didn't.

That is really important, I feel emotional because you have to know this. The emotion I feel is in your heart (talking about the needle sensation in the back of my heart).

I feel a lot of heat in my crown chakra validating that we are on the right track. This is not coming from a weakness inside you. Yes, you have been fighting and it is an enormous battle for you, and this is not the first time you fight this entity. You have been in a psychic war. It is an archetypal, because you are an anointed messenger of the Divine Mother, just like the anointed messengers that were destroyed in the inquisition.

When the Divine Mother fully empowers Her force on this planet, which is happening, it's going to be amazing. We are already seeing it. It is coming along this year.

It is a lot for my mind to even conceive how vast this is. It is incomprehensible, because you are an anointed Messenger of the Divine Mother, you now have the power of Light to face this entity and vanish it from the world. Sending it to the place of All Transformation; yielding it to the light through love, compassion, and forgiveness weakens its structure.

I am going to invoke and spin the Master Key when we enter the mirror of Maria Magdalena to support and sustain your energy in the confrontation that you have to have with him. So now we invoke the living temple of Light in the inner sanctuary of the Soul. As we enter this space of the holiest of the holiest, we open the embodiment of the Divine Feminine God Force that is the resonance, vibration, and power of Oneness that is the Feminine Force of Creation. It is now invoked in co-creation with the Master Force of the Masculine Force of Creation and the Angelic Realms though the Trinity of the Christ, Christ Michael, Christ Magdalena, and Christ Jesus, and now we enter the space of pure divinity of love and light that is the mirror of Maria Magdalena, the mirror of your soul, the Source of Divinity, the Source of Light, and open to the pure vibration of light, the Primordial God consciousness of your soul.

I am that I am. All that I am.

I am made of Love, I am made of Light, I am Oneness.

Stand fully in your light and in your power, for no shadow of fear shall cast darkness upon you. He has no power behind it, and your mind will not give strength.

There is so much light in your heart and in your soul. You are the beauty of that light. It fills you now as never before with the promise of your soul's illumination and the gift of grace.

I am Magdala Yahweh; I am the Feminine Christ.

Kadoish, Kadoish, Kadoish Adonai Tsebayoth. As above, so below. As spirit, so the soul. This shall be manifested in all dimensions, in all realities, and on all aspects of your consciousness, Lucero. So be it, and so it is.

Here is a message from Jesus, The Christ,

> *'Heaven's doors are being opened for you;*
> *I am sending my Light to you ALL.*
> *– I am the Christ.*

I come in the name of God,
I come in the name of Love,
I am here to show you the way to freedom,
to show you the way to me,
to bring yourself back to me,
back to the Father.
Breathe my light—my Golden Light that will nourish your soul.
I am bathing you with this Light;
stay with it.
Go with it everywhere you go.
You are safe. I am with you.
You are an ambassador of Light, of my Light.' "

A few days after this session, I remembered a tarot reading I had with a Venezuelan lady in Sedona. I will never forget the horror-face she made when she saw the cards I had picked. She tried without success to hide her emotions. After a moment of silence, she said: "*You will have a big battle with the dark. But at the end, you shall triumph and be re-born.*" After Judith's session, I comprehended the meaning of her words.

God's Promise

Days after the above session, on a cloudy day, I was inspired to sit by the window where Mother Mary's altar was. As soon as I sat on the floor, the clouds opened up and a column of light from the sun came directly onto me. When it hit me, I saw the cloud of light taking the shape of a Merkaba surrounding me completely. I heard, "*You'll never be harmed.*"

What a powerful demonstration of love and protection.

More Clearing in the Back of My Heart

The discomfort in the back of my heart did not go away completely. I was directed to meditate on it, remembering that the very first time I felt this pain had been two years earlier in Sedona, and how I'd healed at that time. I went deeper to find out that there were more arrows from past-life battles that had been there since then. Using my imagination, I removed a total of seven, filling the punctures with cosmic love and forgiveness. I sent those arrows back to their creators with love, light, and full consciousness. The pain is 95 percent gone. I assume it may take time to completely disappear.

The Last Resource I Used - It Worked

I had found nine stones by my creek. They were polished and pretty. I organized them in a cross shape and slept on them. The discomfort finally left my body.

Healing Psychic Attacks with the Energy of Love

Psychic attacks kept approaching. I did all I knew to send them into the light, but at some point, it seemed like the old teachings had stopped working. I had to find another way. I knew that through love we can conquer any endeavor. It is just very complicated to position yourself in a place of absolute calm and love when you are under attack. Guided by what I would call my Arcturian Angels, I prepared myself in advance.

When the next attack came, I sat comfortably, focusing in my heart and imagining that my body was a machine that generated love and compassion. I was able to let the ego mind out of the picture and visualize myself as a generator. I began generating love and compassion in the form of waves onto everything coming in, out and around me. No fighting, no yelling, no invocations, my own power doing the job. It took my breath away when I saw immediate results. Hard to believe, especially because in the past, frequently it took me more than two hours to do a clearing. In jubilee, I jumped yelling, *"I did it!"*

You may ask how I did that. Well, a generator is a machine that generates power. Imagine your whole body producing and shining the frequency of love and/or compassion (choose one if it is easier). We don't see electricity, but we know it's there. Visualize yourself feeling the energy of love brightening from every pore of your wondrous vessel, like a fire blazing fiercely. Practice when you are not under attack. Practice on plants, animals, objects, world situations and so forth. Everything in the universe has consciousness and is usually willing to receive it, but if you want to heal someone, ask permission first. The power of love is so strong that it will work alone. Don't engage the mind, just your heart.

More Tests of Initiation—A Snake

I kept receiving great opportunities to use the practice of love as a weapon/tool/gift, whatever you want to call it, to heal situations.

One evening, I opened the front door of the cabin to find a long, black snake entering the deck through the stairs. I stayed calm by the door, looking at her, opening my heart, and pouring love into her. She kept moving toward my door, and I continued the process. Luckily, I was standing behind the screen door! She rested by the window. I ran and closed it. I closed the door and went back inside. When I came back, she was gone.

Another test—more difficult, perhaps—occurred when a mosquito or flea bite me seven times while sleeping. The pain was agonizing. I covered the bites with magnesium oil, which provoked an unimaginable burning sensation, then I put on lemon. I tried desperately to get rid of the discomfort once and for all, until I discerned that I had to apply LOVE. I sat against a wall and filled each one with waves of love. After a few days of doing this, the pain went away. The worst part of all was that every time I went outside, mosquitoes bit me in such an outrageous way, I gave up the wilderness and stayed inside until I left the cabin for good.

The Power of Forgiveness

I must admit that uncovering the truth caused me excruciating pain. I am not an exception to the rule. I am a human being just like any other. I cried and went numb for a while in victimland, trying to discern the whys.

The material world inflicted me with so much pain and agony that I sailed away from my True Self. Nonetheless, the Divine Me pushed so strongly that I could not help but acknowledge it moving me in the right direction—my own God self. My early lifestyle had lost all its appeal, and my heart was desperate to reconnect with Divine Source.

The process of forgiveness and acceptance has been my gateway to Oneness. It made me realize that my seemingly undeserved suffering was my own creation and that life is nothing but a marvelous opportunity for evolution and growth. Our biggest challenge is to break the illusion of the material world to see our own radiance. Then, and only then, are we able to transmute suffering into wisdom, and hatred into compassion. At the end, these experiences of separation created a humbler and more powerful version of me, for which I am deeply grateful. Although the process of healing can be traumatic, it can be our greatest ally in the long run. It allows us to show benevolence to our attackers, for they are prisoners of their own minds and of their own traumas.

In 2015, Master Jesus gave me a lovely suggestion: "*Go to the mountains, go in solitude.*" Later, He said: "*Leave all behind and follow me.*"

The Himalayan experience infused me with the courage to disentangle my drama and jump into the unknown. Subsequently, in January 2018, following Master Jesus' recommendations, I moved into a small cabin surrounded by the Smoky Mountains of North Carolina. There, I followed an almost monastic, solitary lifestyle, listening to my own soul, isolated from the world, praying, fasting, detoxing, writing, doing vows of silence, meditating, offering healings, communing with Mother Nature. Living my most intimate desires in union with the divine, I found solace my soul was crying for.

The sound of silence is a great ally to merge with our divine self completely.

My time there was the most glorious and also the most convoluted. Facing oneself is one of the most complex trials a human being may experience. Clearing emotions, negative beliefs and attachments through inner work, as well as fighting alone against the dark, is a very compelling yet formidable experience. Of course, the divine support is always available if your higher self allows it. When solo, one has to learn to listen to his/her intuition in order to resolve the most insignificant test. The spiritual battles continue, but their intensity has diminished. In these last years of meditation and learning, I have become a much calmer person. I rarely lose control or get hysterical. However, in this solitude, I have found myself screaming and kicking when I've been against the wall. Of course, my Masters rushed to help, providing me with alternatives. I am humbled and incredibly grateful to the Divine for teaching me how to open my heart into total, unconditional love and Oneness for All that Is.

I live drinking from the grail of love, the grail of light, the grail of peace that God offers me constantly. I am inviting you to join me. I found my purpose and I am incessantly living it. What is the secret? I would say the only secret resides within. The fountain of ecstasy is already in the confines of our being. We spend our lives trying desperately to obtain material possessions and, when they come, we spend the rest fighting to keep them. Those belongings are secondary, for without an open heart, we can never find real satisfaction on Earth. Struggling to "become someone," we step out of our true essence and forget our most intimate desires, shutting down our pains instead of facing them. The time has come for us to lift the veil of illusion and see our real beauty, to be our own master.

I invite you to browse through these pages and be contaminated with my enthusiasm. Later in this book I have included a guide to unlock your potential. It shows the steps that led me to my awakening. I hope they inspire you to release the chains through your inner work.

I truly believe that, at this moment, we are getting out of our shells, opening to the truth that we are Multidimensional Beings Living A Human Experience by choice.

As I needed to move forward, I listed my cabin for sale. Nothing happened for three months. When I asked why it was taking so long, I only heard: *"Finish writing."* I kept doing it. When I had concluded all writing, I received an offer. Forty days later, I left the cabin to continue my journey somewhere else.

CHAPTER V
YOUR LIBERATION

This spectacular photo shows a spiral of light coming from the sun. It seems like it is joining the reflection on the lake. Can you see the starship on top of the spiral?

"Open your heart, expand it.
Let the power within you flow.
Your heart contains all that you have been longing for.
Allow love, allow joy, and you will be the creator of
your own life.
There is a blazing flame within you.
Dare yourself to ignite it.
Recognize your own power.
Dare to believe in yourself!"

All Your Wishes Are Attainable

It was shocking for me to learn that God lives in our hearts and that we just need to break the bondages of our obliviousness to live in a paradise of joy and richness!

Based on that awareness, I have arranged a set of practices to declutter our precious source of wealth, the heart. A constant practice would inject you with a torrent of stamina and resilience to face whatever the day brings. God's greatest desire is to see us free from the illusion of lack and oppression. Let's become a beacon of light, a symbol of love, an emanation of pure heart energy by bringing more joy into our lives. Joy is a synonym of abundance.

Step One: Grounding Exercise

Being grounded means being present in the body and connected with our beloved Mother Earth. This allows us to stay centered and strong like a mountain; whatever happens around will not influence our state of being because we are balanced. On the opposite side, when ungrounded we are like leaves floating in the wind, and it is easy to be thrown out of balance. Check the exercise below.

Step Two: Gratitude Exercise

Gratitude is an elevated emotion that assists us to happily stay in touch with our inner selves. Dedicate a few minutes each day to write down at least ten things for which you are grateful. Embed that feeling within; sense its energy throughout your body. During the day, repeat in your mind: *"I am grateful for being alive,"* *"I am grateful I can breathe,"* or whatever phrases inspire you. Begin by thanking yourself for having the audacity to follow this or any other freedom process.

Step Three: Forgiveness Therapy

By forgiving others, we may heal many traumas that are keeping us down. As a result, we attract more joy and abundance into our lives. You deserve to get those ordeals out of your system. Don't let blame, guilt or shame steal your happiness. Use the powerful practice in this chapter. Use the same method to forgive yourself, too! It will give you more harmony, because you will be loving yourself more and more. Don't procrastinate—do it for yourself. You don't need to talk to your trespassers if you don't feel like it. This process is for your own well-being. You deserve it.

Step Four: Recognize Your Attachments and Let Them Go

Did you know that gambling, alcohol, food, television, an unpleasant job environment, a relationship that we internally dislike, and traumas create attachments that keep us away from our dreams? We all have fallen into that trap in one way or another. But little by little, we can release them. To get started, you need to be brutally honest with yourself to identify what your cravings are. What are those things you need to do every day or every weekend that, if you don't do them, make you feel different? Each trauma, pain, or disease has its counterpart in the emotional system. If a person felt abandoned or rejected growing up, it is very likely that a fear of being abandoned or rejected will keep reflecting on his/her relationships, leading him to be extremely controlling and insecure. Holding an addiction may make her/him feel safe. Therefore, the sense of insecurity needs attention in order to attract more organic relationships. How do we heal that? Keep reading—the next step is vital.

Step Five: Meditate

In order to take control of our lives and let go of attachments, we need to be in control of our ego minds. How? Through daily meditation. Start with ten minutes, increasing it little by little. Meditation provides us with self-confidence, a sense of invincibility that, in turn, assists us to be in control of our emotions without external additives. All the answers reside within. Your higher self will provide you with the strength necessary to cut your attachments. It takes practice, but it works. There are meditations included below.

Step Six: Include Visualizations in Your Meditations

While in a deep state of meditation, envision yourself having the life of your dreams while being joyful and blissful at the same time. Be sure you are feeling the peace and joy those dreams may bring to you. Put your left hand on your heart area to make it more real and hold it for as long as you can. Follow it daily until you see results.

Step Seven: Self-Love Exercise—Healing the Inner Child

This should be a daily practice. Giving love to yourself enriches your life. The "Healing the Inner Child" meditation is extremely powerful. Both practices will raise your vibration, assisting you to keep a positive attitude toward your development. Watch your negative thoughts and change them to those that ignite your purpose. Use positive affirmations and hang them throughout your house to stay tuned in. Re-training your thoughts with the power of your heart will be helpful during the process as well.

Step Eight: Heal Relationships

Do you feel like you want to change the world? Perfect. Start by changing yourself, and everything around you will begin to mirror you. Because we cannot change others, we may inspire them, but only through our own behavior. I invite you to follow the process for more peace and calm in your life.

Step Nine: Journaling

Journal your feelings and your experiences during this process. And, more importantly, write beautiful things to whomever inspires you. Just write whatever makes you happy. If you don't like what you wrote, start over until you are satisfied.

Step Ten: Work Out—Daily, if Possible

Any type of cardio, yoga, qi-gong, or tai-chi would be appreciated by your being and will maintain your motivation.

Step Eleven: Fasting, Detoxifying the Body

Read about the process and benefits of fasting and detoxifying the body. If you feel the call, go for it. It is extraordinarily powerful. If you have medical issues, ask your doctor for instructions. My personal doctor is my heart. I ask all sorts of questions, and the heart never ever goes wrong. It contains infinite wisdom.

General Recommendations

Set Boundaries—Make the decision to step away from what is silently keeping you hostage. Allow the power of the heart to change your present dead life to a new vibrant and joyful one. A life that makes you jump out of bed every day with new ideas, with new creations, constantly expanding with a permanent sense of satisfaction while helping others to wake up at the same time.

Avoid Over Giving— I don't mean just in the material sense. Be cautious, avoid giving your power away. Don't allow people or things to dictate your life and behavior.

The goal is to keep the spark of God within us constantly ignited. What we have been looking for outside is already within. Once we acknowledge our divinity, we will stop banging our heads against the wall and blaming ourselves or others for our misfortunes. In other words, we will be in control of our lives and become creators rather than victims.

Ask yourself this question: Where have I been? Have I given my power away through habits, cravings or addictions? Reunite with your soul by noticing your own light, your own beauty. A simple exercise of breathing can assist us greatly. Breathe deeply more frequently. Did you know that each breath gives us life, and that by being constantly aware of it, we may increase our chances of being happier, healthier, and wealthier? Each breath can be a wasted one or an encouraging one—we choose. Choose life by appreciating all things and people around you. Avoid self-criticism—we all make mistakes, but our efforts to be better are more important than criticizing ourselves. Follow the steps mentioned above and, if you go back to old behaviors, gently start over. Begin falling in love with yourself!

Let's Get Started!

Please read every meditation first to familiarize yourself with it. Avoid driving or operating any machine during the process.

Practices & Meditations

Exercise 1. Grounding

Standing or sitting, breathe deeply a few times focusing on your body. Imagine roots coming out of your feet going down, down to the core of the Earth. Imagine her filling those roots with loving energy. Then, visualize them returning to you, up through your legs and staying in the root chakra, holding you, keeping you grounded. Every time you feel out of balance, repeat this exercise, it is easy and quick.

Exercise 2. The Power of Gratitude

The following is a great message about gratitude. I received it in Spanish; however, I did my best to interpret it into English.

"I am Divine Mother, I come in the name of truth.
I come in the name of Love.
I want you to learn the value of appreciation,
The value of gratitude—appreciate yourself.
Learn to trust yourself,
To love yourself,
To be yourself.
The veil has been lifted—
you can see better now.
The road ahead is clear for you to move on
to your destiny,
to your path.
Forget the worries, focus on yourself.
Never underestimates the power of Love."

Gratitude opens the doors to heaven. It elevates our vibration to a sense of oneness. Besides that, when we are in a state of gratitude, our hearts open exponentially, attracting more of what we are grateful for. I wrote the following as a reminder to thank the Creator for being alive one more day.

GOD MORNING!
I am grateful, I can breathe,
I love each cell of my body,

*I love helping others to find their way back home,
back to YOU.
I love planet Earth.
I love my earthly family,
I love my galactic family.
I love my enemies.
I love my teachers.
I love myself.*

I LOVE YOU!

There are millions of things for which we can be thankful. Being aware of them provides more satisfaction and joy in our lives. I can assure you that this frequency will elevate your consciousness in a very special way. Make an effort to make a list on a daily basis to see a difference in your state of mind.

Exercise 3. Delete Button to Release Unwanted Attachments

Have you noticed how computers delete files? I bet you have! We are very similar to a computer system. We can delete negative programs, false belief systems, harsh emotions and so forth from our system by just clicking the DELETE button with great intention and emotion.

I tried it and it worked! Only one *caveat*: sometimes the unwanted attachments are so embedded in our system, we may need to do it more than once, but it works.

Here it is: Define first what you would like to delete from your system—many things, probably, like me. No problem. You can work on each of them at your own pace. No stress, no appointments, no witness, totally free!

As usual, find a perfect place and time to do it. Once you are aware of the list of things, feelings, emotions and thoughts you don't want to accept in your life anymore, close your eyes, breathe deeply, and connect with your inner being. Visualize a machine that is able to follow your commands (create your own design machine). Say aloud: I want to detach myself from any emotions, feelings, thoughts, memories, fears and anger related to _____. Imagine a machine voice confirming what you just said: Are you sure you want to delete any emotions, thoughts, feelings, memories, anger, fear related to _____? Say out loud: "*Yes!*" Visualize a big red button in front of you that reads: DELETE. Click on it with intention. As soon as you do, imagine a bright light taking a dense pattern around your energy field all the way up to the sky. It is important that you visualize that density in any shape or color you choose being absorbed by the light and going up, up until it becomes impossible to see it. It is gone!

If for any reason you feel those emotions again, repeat the exercise as many times as needed. Just believe it works. Do the same with each person, attachment, vice or situation you wish to release.

Exercise 4. Forgiveness Therapy

> *"Forgiveness comes from the heart,*
> *the heart can override an insult, s*
> *the mind does not know how to forgive.*
> *When you notice that you are trying to prove yourself right,*
> *the mind is taking control,*
> *for the heart does not need to prove anything."*
>
> *Divine Mother*

Forgiveness means liberation, and the more we invest time in our liberation, the closer we get to manifesting our dreams. We all have been through experiences that scream for forgiveness, but we keep ignoring them. I would like to add that after trying many different methods to forgive forever, I ended up creating my own method, which has been amazing. You may use it to forgive yourself or to forgive others one by one.

Get started by making a list of people or events that have caused you pain and work on each one within your own schedule.

First Day:

Begin by writing your story several times. The same story that caused you pain. Write it over and over again. Yes, the same story. Tell the story as if you had an audience in front of you. Allow all the anger, hatred, resentment, sadness, or whatever emotions come out. Yell, scream, kick a punching bag, hit pillows, do anything to release those emotions in a healthy way.

The best part of all is that your heart will tell you when to stop. Basically, when you get sick and tired of repeating the story, and you have reached a point where you feel like saying "Again?" it's time to let it go! Your psyche will agree that you do not need that story anymore; you are ready to stop identifying yourself with that pain. Burn any papers you have written and stop thinking of that story for the rest of the day.

Second Day:

Write a letter of joy and peace, mentioning only positive aspects about the relationship. Express all that you have learned from that experience and how grateful you are. Allow only positive feelings to run through your mind; instill them in your heart.

Here and after every time you think of that event, remember the positive feelings you instilled in your heart and let them take control. Be strong and stick to the vibration of joy and peace that translates into self-love. Transmuting those negative feelings of victim consciousness into joy and peace is a sign that you care for yourself, that you love yourself, and that you are in charge of your emotions. Nobody can hurt you again, because you have the ability to transmute any negativity into light and joy for your own well-being. You don't need to talk to your trespassers if you don't feel like it. You are doing this exercise for you because YOU ARE THE MOST IMPORTANT PERSON in this world. Don't forget that.

Step Two of Second Day:

You have done a marvelous job. Now get comfortable, relax, close your eyes, breathe deeply, focus in your heart, and picture two cherubim angels pouring a jar of golden liquid light through your crown chakra onto every cell, atom, organ, tissue of your body. Feel the peace and joy this light gives you. Don't open your eyes until you experience those feelings throughout your entire body. When you do, smile and give yourself a hug for having the courage to set yourself free. Wait a few minutes before going back to normal life and don't forget to get rid of the paper on which you wrote your story.

Henceforth, when you feel wounded by someone or a traumatic event happens in your life that gets you out of balance, repeat this exercise. It is easy, simple, and free! Your own wisdom has cleared your grief. Congratulations!

Exercise 5. Meditations

Opening your Heart

Find a comfortable place where you cannot be disturbed, close your eyes, relax the body from the top or crown chakra to your feet. Breathe slowly, resting your attention in the heart center. Feel, listen to the rhythm of your heart, your palpitations, and focus on them.

Once you are very relaxed, visualize a beautiful flower in the chest area opening its petals, and notice how you are feeling. Is there any uneasiness or agitation there? If there is, breathe slowly, focusing on whatever you notice. Keep connecting with your heart; that will open the door to your divinity. At the beginning, it may seem like you are doing nothing, but that nothingness is what you need at the time. If you are going through any situation that confuses you, take this opportunity to ask your heart questions. You may hear, sense or visualize the answer, or you will probably find the answer through someone, a book, or even a television show or movie. Adopt this practice as a part of your life; it assists in keeping the heart open and receptive to your spiritual needs. During the day, if you need to make a decision, make the effort to breathe and connect again. You will be surprised to see how things change around you.

Maintain an Open Heart

Following the above exercise, while your heart opens like a flower, imagine a golden light coming from it directly into each child on Earth, into those who may feel lonely, abandoned, hopeless, ill, imprisoned, abused, or lost. Let your imagination fly and see yourself full of light, travelling and reaching all those places where light and love are needed the most. Bless them, pour your heart into them, allow joy and good to emanate from your being. You are a powerful being of light. You can do this and much more. Allow your imagination to guide you. Keep your heart open and your light on while doing this. Explore more ways to assist humanity, let your imagination take you to places you never thought of, always full of light. Giving without expecting anything in exchange is a potent practice. Allow your divine nature to fully guide you, integrate with this energy, do your best to stay in a joyful mode. When you feel complete, stay still for a while, thanking yourself and the universe for assisting others. It is an honor to be of service.

Creating Coherence between Brain and Heart

Get comfortable. Find a place where you are cannot be interrupted. Close your eyes, make no effort to control your breathing. Let it simply follow its natural rhythm. If your mind keeps thinking, gently go back to your breathing. Once you feel more relaxed, focus your attention in your heart. Imagine and visualize a flow of pink light coming from your heart, swirling and filling your brain with this stream of light. The brain receives it with gratitude and sends it back to the heart, increasing the feeling of appreciation. It is important that you sense it and augment it—expand it. Keep going back and forth—heart-brain-brain-heart, visualizing it in a very calm, relaxing way that connects them like two old friends meeting again after a long separation. Stay tuned into that state of peace and appreciation for the rest of your day.

Exercise 6. Add Visualizations to Your Meditation Practice

Being Grateful in Advance is a practice that helps manifest your dreams. First: Make a list of the things you wish to have.

Second: Relax yourself by breathing deeply, resting your attention in your heart area. Third: Envision yourself receiving your dreams. Let's suppose that the doorbell rings. You open the door, and the mail person is there holding those gifts for you. How would you feel? Grateful? Joyful?

Fourth: Focus on the frequency of gratitude and let it run through your whole system. Spend time doing that—feeling grateful and joyful for getting exactly what you expected. Feel the emotion of joy through your whole body—the longer the better.

Repeat this exercise daily until you see results. Important: the key is to maintain a feeling of gratitude as if it had already happened and allow the universe to work. We can do magic—we only need to believe we can.

Exercise 7. Self-Love Exercise

Divine Mother insists that Self-Love is a vital part of our awakening, as well as the foundation to attract more love into our lives. By loving yourself, you can recognize how lovely and mighty you are. The following is a great exercise to help you stay in this frequency.

As soon as you wake up in the morning, connect with that amazing vortex of love that has the power to change your life: your heart. Breathe deeply and rest your attention in the heart area. As you do, give yourself a hug and begin telling yourself all those things that you wish to hear from others, such as: "_____ *(your name), you are such a wonderful mom or dad. You are an amazing human being. You are nice and lovable. You are a great teacher, an incredible journalist. I am very proud of you. I love you, I love you, I love you.*" You can go on and on for as long as you wish, as it is never too much. Self-Love should be a daily practice for every human being. You may go further and teach your children and others to do the same. During the day, don't accept judgment or criticism about you, especially self-criticism. Just talk in a gentle way to yourself, and soon you will be talking like that to others. If someone tells you something negative about your behavior, look that person in the eye and say: "*I am a nice and goodhearted person,*" or whatever statement may fit the situation. Remember, you are a wonderful being of light.

Healing the Inner Child

Did you know that a wounded inner child can ruin many aspects of our lives without being noticed?

The inner-child figure is a powerful aspect of our lives that needs to be healed so we can continue to grow and evolve with ease and grace. The following is a meditation I was inspired to do on my clients and myself with excellent results.

<u>Step 1</u>. Relax, slowly breathe into your heart, keep your focus on it.

<u>Step 2</u>. Evoke memories of your childhood. See yourself as a child. Go back as far as possible; without rushing, bring forth memories that might have caused you anxiety or pain, confusion, anger, or any uncomfortable emotion. Select any of them and feel the emotions you went through at that time.

<u>Step 3</u>. Visualize a little child in front of you. Look at her/him carefully. Are they feeling abandoned, rejected, sad, lonely, or perhaps hungry? Can you express compassion toward this child? Can you give them a hug? I am hoping you can. if you cannot, just stop the process and wait until you are ready without self-judgment.

<u>Step 4</u>. If you are ready to move forward, give him/her a hug while saying: "*I love you. I am sorry that you are going through this situation, but I promise that from now on I will be with you and will take care of your needs, fears, phobias, and anything you may need. You will never be alone again, I am with you*". Imagine your heart fully open and the child jumping into your heart with a smile on their face. Put your hands on your heart area and welcome

them into the wholeness of your heart. Say as many times as you wish: "*I love you, now we will be united forever*".

Step 5. What did you enjoy doing when you were little? Maybe running down the hill with the wind blowing against your face? How about that special food or that special place? Whatever it was, promise your inner child that you both are going to spend time doing that. It could be just once or twice a month if your schedule is tight, or as many times as possible.

Step 6. Take your inner child to do the activities you promised. It is very important to keep the relationship alive so that you don't fall into the same situation again. If your inner child is happy, nothing can stop you from being happy too. If you have gone through traumatic situations in your adult life, it may be something that was bothering your inner child that has been unattended.

Exercise 8. Relationships

>You are opening into the truth and
>When you see from the level of truth
>You will see the beauty that is occurring
>In, out and around you.
>Learn to look with your heart.
>Use the eye in your heart to see that beauty!

Every Relationship Is a Blessing

This is a mighty meditation that heals with the power of love, especially for those times we have disagreements or conflict with someone we love and wish to be at peace with but, for some reason, we don't dare ask for forgiveness, or we have a hard time forgiving.

Situate yourself in a relaxed position, breathing deeply at the beginning to connect with the power of your beautiful heart. Slow down your breath while focusing on your heart area; close your eyes and visualize the person you are having trouble with in front of you. Visualize green light coming from your heart into his/her chest area. Call their name and say slowly: "*I love you, I love you, I love you.*" See the light coming from your heart into the other person's heart. Repeat it as many times as you wish.

This seems like a simple exercise, but it is extremely powerful. My first experience was amazing. The other person sent the light back to me, assuring me that she also loved me, and that nothing could keep us apart. At a deep soul level, we love one another. What we see with our physical eyes is just an illusion, the illusion that we have chosen to experience.

> *"Relationships allow us to learn about Love, and*
> *the healing power that it holds.*
> *However, whatever conflict or pain we hold inside*
> *will be mirrored in those relationships.*
> *Only in forgiving and loving ourselves, our past and present*
> *may we trust enough to freely love another.*
> *Trust of another is based on trusting your own self."*
>
> *Divine Mother*

A Sweet Recommendation—Blessings

Blessings will be showered on you without extreme efforts, and it is so contagious, it may create a powerful web of love and elation that would help us stick together into a new world of peace. All together as ONE, creating a new generation, helping each other without competition or selfishness, in constant unity. Every day, bless yourself and bless others without exception, especially those you don't like. Bless the Earth and humanity unconditionally. This is an extraordinary practice that reverts back to you in an indefinable way.

Exercise 9. The Importance of Journaling

There are many reasons to begin journaling your experiences. First of all, it helps you to be more in touch with your inner self, enhancing your sense of well-being. It helps you reduce stress and boost your mood, clearing your mind. Take a few minutes a day to record your thoughts and emotions—this will lead to knowing yourself better and be clear about situations and people who are toxic for you. Even if you are angry or sad, write about it and it will help you reduce the intensity of those feelings.

On the other hand, it is advisable for your heart to keep another small journal to write from your soul. Write poems or love letters—anything that elevates your frequency and makes you feel merrier.

Exercise 10. Work Out

Aim for at least 30 minutes of physical activity daily. Do your best to find the time for some regular, vigorous exercise for extra health and fitness benefits as well as improvement of memory. Try martial arts. It provides great mental clarity and a sense of invincibility that keeps negative thought forms away.

Exercise 11. The Power of Fasting—Detoxifying the System

The impact of fasting is so inspiring that one cannot help but acknowledge it. It assists us in reaching a deeper connection with the Divine. The soul comes to join the personality to create a humbler and more harmonious you by falling into an absolute state of grace by overcoming the controlling mind. The benefits are endless. I truly believe that each being has different reactions according to their higher self. Before a fasting and detox process, meditate on it; ask for guidance to find the best approach for you.

More Loving Suggestions

Massaging the Brain to Release Stress

At times, we can get stressed out by the obligations and survival responses we have to confront daily, which makes it harder to stay calm and in control. This exercise will assist you in quickly calming your brain and will provide you with strength and motivation in exchange.

You can literally do this exercise anywhere. It takes three minutes. Relax and inhale through your nose. Focus on the heart. Gently exhale through the mouth. Push the air up to the face, to the forehead and back through the brain, like combing it, and letting it go. Do it again at least three times. You will feel a big difference. It works marvelously.

Retrain Your Thoughts with the Power of the Heart to Change Your Reality

Now that you know how to create coherence between your heart and brain, you may want to go further and educate your mind into positive thinking.

While in a meditative state, keep your attention in the heart area. Visualize a radiant, blazing, powerful golden light igniting in your heart center, going up to your mind, and filling your thoughts. Make it as clear, visual, and real as possible. Remember that the heart is the one doing the job. Don't try to analyze what is the mind and what is the brain. If you feel that visualizing the brain may be easier, do it like that. Just keep following the sequence, the heart nourishing your mind, like you are inflating a balloon going up to the mind from the heart. The Infinite Wisdom of the heart is doing the job. Keep allowing the heart to fill the mind with this powerful, golden light. Now, tell your mind: "*I love you, I love you, I love you. We are going to work together with love and compassion. The heart is in charge now; you just need to listen to it.*" Tell your mind nice things but in a commanding voice. The heart is in control.

Throughout the day when a negative thought comes forth, such as: "*I am tired of that diet; I'd rather eat pizza,*" change that thought and say: "*Wait, I am not tired of my diet. I love it; I love eating healthy.*" And go for your healthy diet. Remember how good it feels to look fit and healthy. Hence, nurture your mind with positive thinking, retrain it. Your heart has the power to change anything in your lifestyle. Keep doing it and, little by little, you will see your mind supporting the goals you always wanted to achieve. Also, talk to your mind in a gentle but firm way: "*Don't worry, mind. We are having a positive view of life, and everything is perfect.*" Tell your mind how much you love it and how grateful you are for its services, and that working along with the heart, you can achieve anything! This will bring more joy into your life, and you will be more satisfied and happier with your own self.

This practice works beautifully. I began noticing positive outcomes in my life. I felt a deep sense of freedom and had the courage to make decisions I knew deep inside I had to follow but that my own resistance had made me believe were unattainable. My life changed exponentially. Yours can too!

The Heart Is a Generating Love Machine

As a generator of love and light, the heart contains infinite wisdom. Based on that statement, I have arranged practices that can provide you with anything you wish as long as you hold a good intention.

Researchers have proven that the heart is 100x more powerful electrically, and up to 5,000x more powerful magnetically than the brain. The heart actually sends more messages to the brain than the brain does to the heart. Our hearts actually "think", and have neural tissue, hence the term "heart intelligence." The heart's magnetic field, which is the strongest rhythmic field produced by the body, not only envelops every cell, but also extends out several feet in all directions around us.

Before Leaving the House

This is what I called "paving the way" because it is literally like paving the way for you with love and light. Before leaving the house, close your eyes and extend your arms. Visualize light coming from your heart and saturating a road in front of you—the road you will be driving on. Now, decree the following: *"I send out a path of divine light onto each road I may be driving on today, keeping me protected and secure at all times. So be it, it is done."* It works like magic.

At a Public Place

Before getting into any place you visit or work, find somewhere you can close your eyes. If you cannot close your eyes, just imagine the light coming from your heart and filling, bathing, saturating every person you may encounter during your day as well as every place you go, whether a store, hospital, office, or your workplace. Surround everybody with that light—your boss, co-workers, clients, you name it. I do it frequently, and life becomes heaven wherever I go!

Dissolving a Traffic Jam with Love!

During a terrible traffic jam on I-95, I felt this need to bless every car and every person in every car, unconditionally, exceedingly, and without exception. Then I poured divine light into all of them. It was an amazing experience, and the traffic dissipated almost immediately. Later, I was inspired to do the same, but this time to bless and fill all their families, friends, neighbors, enemies, and so forth with divine light. It feels so good to do that. You feel a sense of doing good unto others. It opens the heart. Once, I intentionally pictured myself getting on top of the road, blessing all. It was a really nice experience and so rewarding. You can see results right in front of your eyes. It is an exciting adventure, just try it.

In Oneness with Gaia

Close your eyes. Relax your body. Relax your mind. Breathe deeply, focusing on your heart. Imagine your breath as a stream of light going down, down through your whole body, down through your legs, through your feet, all the way to the core of the Earth—slowly, no rush. Once there, hold your breath for a few seconds and exhale with a loud "*Ahh*," releasing any tension into Mother Earth. Keep breathing, repeating it as many times as you feel is needed. Then bring this energy back up. Use your breath again. Imagine it going up through your feet, legs, hips, stomach—and resting in your beautiful heart. Now this silver light is filling your being with great joy, peace, a sense of prosperity, of oneness. Feel the love of the Divine Mother caressing you, pampering you. Stay in that state of being for as long as possible, feeling safe and secure in Mother's arms. Maintain those feelings, for they are a passport to happiness.

Bringing Love to Gaia and Her Inhabitants

The following meditation is intended to fill Gaia (Mother Earth) and humanity with the virtues of God for a peaceful planet.

Take this meditation as your play time with the angels and streams of colors with an open heart and an innocent intention. The point here is to do it for fun, without stress or fear of not doing it right. Whichever way you perform it, it will be a gift to Earth and humanity. Just allow all those wonderful emotions to fill your being and, ah, don't forget to smile! Feel the angel in you.

Sit quietly in a place where you can relax without being disturbed; breathe deeply, keeping your focus in the heart area. Relax, and using the power of your imagination, situate yourself on top of the North Pole. Extend your hands down with the intention of sending streams of light to the South Pole. Invite the angels to join you. See them bringing streams of light back and forth. Imagine different colors, each one with a different purpose such as joy, love, peace, abundance, healing, any good intention you can imagine. Feel the joy, the peace, the love; have fun with the angels. They love doing it. Get the angel in you to come out!

Beating Cold Temperatures

I was born in Colombia, where cities are either cold or warm all year long. My hometown is always warm, and so is Florida, where I lived for more than twenty years. I had never experienced cold weather until I moved to North Carolina's mountains, where the low temperatures hit me bad at the beginning. Due to my extreme sensitivity, the air conditioning and central heat were usually off. So, inspired by the Iceman Wim Hof method, I decided to take cold—very cold—baths during the winter. I would fill the tub at night and jump in it the following morning. The fact that my central heat was off made the water ice cold but refreshing. I experienced great relief, because the body holds the same temperature as outside. This exercise allowed me to even have breakfast on the deck without suffering. I survived with portable heaters.

Clearing Negativity in My Computer—Mind Control

One evening, I sat in front of my computer with the intention of continuing my writing. After a few seconds, all sorts of negative thoughts began entering my mind. They came so insistently that it made me ill. I took a break and realized that it was coming from my computer! It had happened before, but I'd never realized it. Grateful for receiving this divine wisdom, I decided to practice a healing session on my Mac. Yes, objects can also carry some type of mind control. I invoked Mother-Father God, Angelic Realm, and the Ascended Masters to join me. I broke structures of untruth and sent into the light whatever energy was there trying to put me down. It took a while to clear it out, but finally I felt the release. Breaking structures of mind control or similar can be done with hand gestures or visualizing it.

My Mac is working much better now. I, however, always block the video camera to avoid any intruders penetrating my energy field. It is time to create consciousness about this type of control.

Getting Bugs out of the House— Insects' Consciousness

I read about this technique somewhere—I don't remember where. I feel I have to share it. Based on the concept that everything in the universe, such as animals, plants, things, and so forth possess consciousness, if we use our intrinsic power, we can communicate with them. For instance, if there are ants in your kitchen, you may try to connect your consciousness with theirs, commanding them to leave your space, for they are not welcome there. The possibilities that they follow your command are very high. I did it and then waited until the next day, and something really great happened. I did not see any ants in my house since then. I invite you to try this and let me know your results.

Clearing Plants

In my cabin's surroundings I found a yellow rose bush. I grabbed a couple of them with their permission to adorn my dining table. At lunch time, I noticed that one of the roses was moving. I got closer to find out that a couple of slug-like larvae were feeding on the leaves. Later, I confirmed that they were causing severe defoliation of the bush. I tried different home-made remedies to clear them out, but none worked.

I decided to use my own energy to clear the plant. During meditation, I visualized the plant in front of me. I projected love energy with the intention of clearing the problem. That was all I did.

Amazingly, when I checked the plant a few days later, the larvae were gone! This means we don't need to use chemicals on our beautiful plants; just our own energy can help them. Make an effort to use your own power next time you face the same dilemma and let me know how it goes.

Vacuum Exercise to Keep a Translucid Energy Field

This is the practice I used to get rid of many little men that chased me in my home when nothing else worked. Those "things" were stubbornly watching over my shoulders to see everything I did.

Choose a place where you will not be disturbed. Begin breathing deeply into your heart. Bring your guardian angels into your awareness and visualize them handing you a golden vacuum that is connected to the power and light of our Father Sun. This device has a great capacity to extract any discordant energies in, out, and around you. Grab it and begin the process of vacuuming from your head, face, neck, chest, all the organs, spinal cord, arms, hands—every part of your body, one by one. Do it slowly, don't rush. Dedicate whatever time is needed. While doing that, imagine that all negativity, density, and darkness around you have been replaced with a golden light that fills you completely. Once you have finished, return the vacuum to your angels and watch them taking it to the sun while dissolving it into nothingness. You are done. Keep visualizing yourself full of golden light, the light of God that never fails, the light of God that always prevails. Thank your angels and yourself for this clearing.

The Dangers of Sugar

Sugar is hard to resist, I admit it. Nevertheless, I feel it is time for us to create conscious awareness about its effects on the human body, especially when it comes to our little ones. I honestly believe that children should be educated about the negative impact sugar has in their systems. This will eventually lead future generations to make an informed decision about diminishing its consumption. Research has shown that the sugar we consume actually feeds candida yeast and other unhealthy organisms hiding in our guts. The more sugar you binge on, the more you feed candida.

A study on rats conducted by researchers had found that a diet high in fructose (another word for sugar) hinders learning and memory by literally slowing down the brain.

There are a number of negative effects of sugar. It causes skin to age faster, and excess sugar is stored as fat, which leads to obesity. Sugar ruins your liver, as an excess of it gets stuck in the organ rather than being eliminated as VLDL cholesterol particles. It lowers immunity and ruins teeth, because refined sugar breaks down enamel and causes tooth decay faster than any other food. The skin breaks out. Feeling bloated is not fun nor sexy and it doesn't make you feel good mentally either, but it's apparently a side effect of too much sugar.

It's up to each one of us whether we continue feeding our emotions with sugar and induce our marvelous children to do that, too. Or should we change and decrease its ingestion little by little? We have the power to decide.

View on Politics—Young Creators

I am not an expert on politics, nor do I pretend to be. However, I feel inspired to add my humble opinion about this topic. The United States is a strong country that stands up as an example for the world. As such, it is in need of making a difference. A young politicians' platform filled with fresh, genial ideas would be a remarkable addition to revolutionize the systems. I would like to ask them to stand up and create a new system that works for the benefit of all, without exceptions.

CHAPTER VI
CHRIST CONSCIOUSNESS

A Photo, a Message, and a Meditation

One morning, I jumped out of my bed inspired to take a picture of the sunrise. I went outside and was able to capture this magnificent one. It transmits powerful energy. Asking for its meaning, I heard: *"Christ Consciousness."*

This is what Yeshua, Jesus the Christ said:

> *"Let this light fill you completely, wrap you as a shield of protection. Merge with it and keep that feeling throughout day and night; use it as needed, as much as you wish. There are many in prison, prisoners of their own limitations. Use it to get out of that prison. This is the light that frees you, the light that connects you with the Mind of God. It dissolves any prison created by the mind—just trust and allow. This light has immense power. Use it like wearing your own clothing each day. Send it to others as well. Use it liberally without restrictions; send it to people, groups, countries, to Mother Earth. It will assist to liberate them from the chains. Expand it at your whim. It is for you. Fill your home, your organs, your mind, your brain to obtain mental clarity for better health, for your well-being, and for the well-being of all humanity. Vibrate with this light, feel it."*

Using the Light of The Christ

This type of meditation has been recommended by Jeshua. Use the light coming in the photograph above to send Christ Consciousness into other people's hearts to ease the relationship. Go into a deep state of relaxation using your breath and keeping the focus in the heart center. Visualize the person you want to have a better relationship with and repeat as many times as you wish the Ho'oponopono Hawaiian mantra: *"I love you. I am sorry. Please forgive me. Thank you."* Combining the light of the Christ Consciousness and the powerful mantra, Ho'oponopono, harmony can be restored in one's life. There is a lot of information about this mantra online for your assistance.

Photograph and a Short Dialogue with Him

I took this lovely photograph in a river in Sedona, Arizona. The sign of the cross grabbed my attention. Let me share another divine message from Sananda, Jesus the Christ.

"I am the heart of Sananda."
Me: *"How far should I go to help others?"*
"Don't let them overtake you,
fill them with light, help them
with an open heart.
If they try to keep you down, by filling them with light,
you are assisting them to ascend as well."
Me: *The heart of Sananda is in my heart;*
my body is trembling, my right-hand shaking,
and the left part of my brain is tingling.
I am weeping. I feel His presence.
Me: *"Are you Sananda?"*
"I am here with you.
I Am that I Am.
You are an ambassador of Light.
I Am the resurrection and the life;
I Am perfection everywhere now."
Me: *"Do you have a message for me or for humanity?"*
"I have many messages.
I come in the name of God;
I am filling you with my light.
Let go of all and any worries.
I want you to feel my presence—stay still."

Devotion

Devotion is the commitment to some purpose; it involves feelings of ardent love. That is how I feel, totally devoted to you, my beloved Mother/Father God. I am grateful for my unwavering devotion! I am grateful for my beautiful life with YOU, Nameless One, Divine Mother, Jeshua, Angelic Realm, the list is never-ending. My life is a garden of love, of flowers, of laughter. I live a dancing life of miracles. I invite you to join me!

One day at 4:37 a.m., while writing in my journal, my right hand began to shake. I received the following message:

"Continue writing;
fill yourself with Christ Consciousness
so nothing can affect you.

Within the Heart of God, I Am

I am Mother-Father God,
Your Creator; this is part of your spiritual growth.
I Am that I Am.
I asked: "What is Christ Consciousness?"
"Christ Consciousness is to acknowledge the Christ within.
It is all about Him and His teachings—His light, His peace,
His love—study His ray—
Messages of love will bring Christ Consciousness on to each person.
By you giving love, you are teaching them
Christ Consciousness—compassion, love, wisdom, joy, and peace."

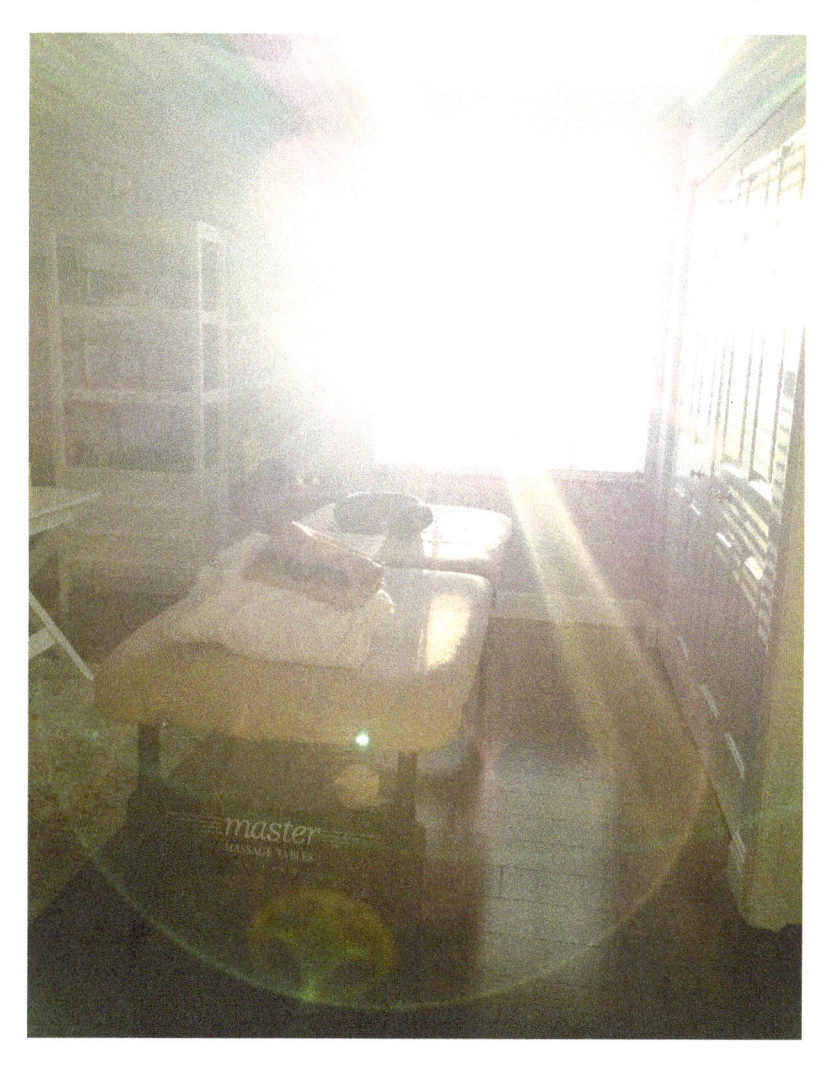

A Fourth-Pointed Star in A Circle

This photograph reflects a four-pointed star hologram that I had never seen before. After that day, it has appeared in many of my photographs. I was overflowing with love, mesmerized by the beauty of the star. When I asked for its meaning, I heard: "*The second coming of the Christ.*" The feelings of peace and joy that it radiates are indescribable. Meditate on these photographs, for they contain powerful soul value.

A short conversation with my Treasured Jeshua, Jesus the Christ:

Me: "I want to open my heart to you, my beloved Jeshua."
He: "I am here, with you.
I am covering you with my Love, with my light.
I am at your right, left, front, back.
I want you to remember your dreams.
Your dreams contain information I want you to have."
Me: "I love you, Yeshua; fill me with your Golden Light,
Fill my family with your powerful Love,
Fill Mother Earth as well."
He: "The flower of Light means that we are
all connected, a grid, a web.
We are ONE."

Mahavatar Babaji

Mahavatar Babaji is an Indian yogi, guru and saint. It is said that he still lives in the Northern Himalayas. He is considered an avatar, a deathless embodiment of the Divine in human form. His given name is unknown; he is only known by the name Mahavatar Babaji. This name was given to him by his disciple, Lahiri Mahasaya, who met him several times between 1861 and 1935. Lahiri Mahasaya's disciples have claimed that Babaji is both ageless and deathless. Many consider him to be a legendary figure rather than the actual person many have reported meeting. There are no known records of his birth or death, and little is written about his childhood. His first message to me appears in Chapter IV.

His Second Message Said: "I Live in Your Heart."

In 2017, he came forth when I was planning to get a cabin in the mountains. He guided me to draw the geographical description of the place I was moving into. Months later, I was stunned to see its precision. In meditation, he transmitted the message: *"I live in your heart."*

He is known in the West primarily through the accounts written in Paramahansa Yogananda's book *Autobiography of a Yogi*. Yogananda wrote that Jesus Christ went to India, where he met with Babaji. He envisioned Babaji's role to be working with Christ to plan spiritual salvation for this age. He believed that Babaji and Christ were in communion, sending out vibrations to inspire nations across the world to renounce evils such as wars, racial hatred and materialism.

Once in the cabin, while meditating, I was staring at a figure of an Egyptian god that had appeared in front of me when suddenly, like a thunder, the presence of Babaji took his place, and I heard:

"Every Beating of Your Heart Is a Remembrance of My Soul"

It touched my heart immensely. What a deep, ecstatic phrase that clutches the reality of our beings. I bow to you in gratitude for all that you have done for humanity. I am humbled to be in your presence and honored by your constant support. I clearly saw him with my third eye. He was wearing a turban.

While writing the above description, I sensed his presence again. My heart opened to him like a flower opening its petals, ready to embrace his exquisite stream of love that travels throughout Infinity.

He takes me on etheric travel, where I am immersed in his flow of love. It is impossible to convey the blissfulness of the moment. I am captivated by the magic of the divine experience. I wonder if it is possible to stay in this state forever. What a profound exaltation of devotion!

We were formless, shapeless, and free of any attachment while flowing and flying together as one being—just one. I was mesmerized by this event and trying to recover from its incredible. I am no longer attached to this reality. I am longing to live in his reality—to be one with him. I am in you, and you are in me. Eternal love.

My beloved Master: I wish to reunite with you in eternity, for it is within perpetuity that we find our essence, our real beings uniting with the divine, allowing its substance to nurture our souls. We became enthralled in a vortex of love without the barriers of time-space, in a spiral of light, a spark that reverberates from heart to heart, forming One.

As I put my hand on his picture, I cried. I tried to describe the feeling within the symphony of my heart but could not find the words. I could merely stutter: "*I love you, Babaji!*"

Cobra Breath

I would say that Babaji inspired me to practice the Cobra Breath. This type of breath has the power to open the Shushumna column, which is an invisible funnel that runs parallel to the spinal cord and fills the whole system with light. It is like an explosion within. It is used to expand consciousness, and it can lead to states of bliss and joy. After witnessing its benefits, I would like to recommend it. If you feel the call, experiment with it and research it online. There is a video I like called: "Way of no Way" by a young man. This type of breath played an important role in my awakening. It is said that you can transform your life with just three cosmic Cobra Breaths a day. The incredible impact the Cobra Breath can have on your personal and spiritual growth is the reason it is known as Babaji's gift to humanity.

It stimulates multidimensional change in your being in a powerful yet grounded manner. It quickens the body's circulation as well as in the pineal and pituitary glands. It is said that just one Cobra Breath is equal to one year of meditation. Go forth and practice it to see, to feel a difference in your life. We all have the same potential to manifest what we have been longing for ages. We must trust the unknown and step out of a monotonous life.

The Story of Sanat Kumara—A Planetary Logos

Sanat Kumara—Training a Planetary Logos. This book is the story of Sanat Kumara, the Planetary Logos for the Earth. Master Wyamus says that, thanks to the Planetary Logos' efforts and great wisdom, Earth is able to "walk in great beauty." He explains how one becomes a Planetary Logos, who is an administrator for the Earth, rather like a president. He began just as you and I did with an awareness of himself as light. Over the eons, he moved within that light, enjoying the magnificent colors, playing with and being instructed by the angels and other teachers. It is an amazing text. His work is remarkable. Reading his book was the most extraordinary teaching experience ever. I recommended it to anybody interested in excelling in her/his powers.

Spiral of Light from Sanat Kumara's Book

I obtained this exercise from Sanat Kumara's book. The moment I tried it, my vibration was raised instantaneously. Let's practice it. Close your beautiful eyes and put your attention on the heart area. Begin picturing a spiral of golden light coming from your heart and moving strongly but smoothly through your whole body—the room, the place where you are. Extend it to your town, your county, your state, your country, and onto the whole universe. Play with it. Put colors in it if you feel like it. Move it around to the special places or people you wish to help (schools, hospitals, military offices, violent places, and so forth—use your imagination). Prior to this, I had been questioning: *"Do I have to travel to faraway places to feel Oneness?"* This is the answer I received: *"God is not wherever you go. God is wherever you are. He is within you forever—always in the heart—not in a specific place."* Meditating on Oneness one may travel distances using the spiral of light without moving the physical body.

Oneness Vision

After following an incredible meditation guided by Archangel Metatron, but still in that place of stillness, a huge, striking ball of light brighter than the sun shining in its undefinable beauty appeared before me. In its immensity, it would have been impossible to measure its size by the human eye. It was mesmerizing, brilliant, radiant—the most sparkling golden light ever imagined.

As I stared at it, this impressive light absorbed me without any warning! I was petrified! I wanted to see around, to ask its meaning, when all of a sudden it started swallowing all around me, every human, the moon, the sun, the stars. I saw with my heart beating as hard as I could how it absorbed the whole planet! Then, before I could react, all the planets were in there, other galaxies, all our brothers from other dimensions—everything, until nothing was left! I was disturbed yet amazed by this incredible display! At some point, I couldn't take it any longer and I opened my eyes. I was trembling, mesmerized by the realism of this vision. I could only get into bed holding my legs and shuddering and weeping uncontrollably. It was so intense, yet clear, and I could not get the event out of my mind for days.

Later in meditation, I received that the meaning of the vision was that WE ARE ALL ONE. The Powerful Circle of Radiant Light was nothing else but a potent sphere of ONENESS. It gave me peace to know that there was nothing to worry about, for there was no war, no crime, no negativity that could change the truth of who we are and forever shall be—ONE with ALL THAT IS. I would say that the message was to stay in unity and remember that we are all made of the same fabric.

In Honor of Archangel Michael

Michael, my powerful bodyguard, spiritual protector, guide, confidante, and best friend has dealt with me for all these years of darkness. He has triumphantly taken me out of it with his great deal of support and unconditional love. He has been my constant companion, assisting me in every situation.

My Story with Archangel Michael

Since 2011, while getting to know my way around the spiritual world, I heard constantly that lightworkers worked with Archangel Michael. I was so intrigued about that and pondered how they'd done it and what kind of process or studies one would need to do the same. Fortunately, to my surprise, one does not need any special training or studies, for he comes forth anytime we call for his brilliant assistance. I began calling on him and, to my amazement, he showed up right away!

Allow me to share a story with you. In 2012, I was living in a two level-home. My room was on the first floor, and I had set up a room upstairs for my new-born granddaughter. I had a CD player in her room. One night when nobody was staying upstairs, I woke up at 1:30 a.m. with my heart beating faster than normal. When I heard the CD playing upstairs, I was paralyzed with terror, and the only thing I could mumble was *"Archangel Michael, Arcturians, please help me."* As soon as I said that, the music stopped, and I saw a shade of light leaving my room. Since that day, I began calling for him and, of course, for the Arcturians, whenever I am in need. He is ready to serve anybody at any time. He has played an important role in my spiritual development. Without his guidance, patience and unconditional love, my awakening would have probably been exhaustingly longer.

Another story. In 2015, during a session with a lady called Shekinah Rose in Sedona, Arizona, she was amazed that he appeared so clearly that she literally saw him. He wanted to give me his blue flame sword of truth to fight negativity. He knew I would need it for the time to come, which were the most difficult ones. I had the honor of getting closer to him through one of his dedicated channels: Kelly Hampton, through whom he wrote the book, *Into the White Light*.

I would like to honor a prayer from this wonderful book in which Michael says: *"This is the prayer I wish humanity would say every morning when they awake. This prayer is the essence of life on Earth."*

> *"Nothing is more powerful than the word of God.*
> *Nothing is more beautiful than the word of God.*
> *Nothing is as sacred as the word of God."*
>
> —Archangel Michael

He added another prayer:

> *"Our Father, humble Father of greatness and light,*
> *You and You alone are the source of my power and comfort.*
> *No one, no power, no entity may enter me, for I dwell in your kingdom for now and for eternity.*
> *If I asked you, God, for love, you would give it.*
> *If I asked you, God, for protection, you would give it.*
> *If I asked you, God, for compassion, you would give it.*
> *No one has your power or your grace."*
>
> *Amen.*

During an angel reading session with Kelly Hampton, around November 2014, I felt this urge to decipher who I had been in past lives. So, besides other questions, I asked Archangel Michael at the end of the session:

> *Angel, Who Am I?*
> *I heard:*
> *"Saint Luke, the Apostle."*

His answer perplexed me, left me speechless, very confused. Kelly did not hear my voice for a few minutes. She kept asking: *"Are you OK?"* I just could murmur a yes.

For days, I could not get that out of my mind. I have been trying to accept it and live with it. This is the first time I've shared this. I know you may think that I have lost my mind, but I am as surprised as you. If I am saying this now, it is because God has determined that this is the time to share it, this is a time of awakening, and it may be of help for others like me who have been receiving divine messages but have been afraid to share them with the world. This is the time to get out of the closet and show who we really are.

So far, I don't know how this truth is going to affect my life or what I am supposed to do, but for sure I will do my best to honor St. Luke's name.

"Dear and Glorious Physician"

The book, *Dear and Glorious Physician,* by Taylor Caldwell tells the story of the life of Saint Luke. In fact, she dedicated 48 years of her life to research for this book. His real name was Lucanus—Luke for short. Lucanus was a magnificent physician who performed great healings while on Earth. While reading this book, a swirl of emotions inundated my being. I identified myself with many of his attitudes toward life. I could not avoid weeping, absorbed by the reality of the stories.

CHAPTER VII
DIVINE MOTHER

A Symbol of the Divine Feminine Force of God

"I am Divine Mother,
I come in the name of God,
I come in the name of truth.
I want you to know that you have my support,
My love, my warmth.
Be you, no matter what is going on around you.
Be you, just BE.
There are many things coming to you.
Open the door—the door of your trust,
The door of your belief.
"I open myself to believe in myself."
That is an affirmation to repeat daily,
To encrypt in your psyche, in your skin."

She also suggested the following daily affirmations:

I am worthy of being heard.
I can help others with my story.
I am valuable.
Nobody can hurt me.
I am a powerful being of Light.

Who Is Divine Mother?

Divine Mother is the feminine aspect of Mother-Father God. Divine Mother and God are one. Divine Mother is the creator—she gave birth to creation. God comes to us at this time in the shape of a Mother. The feminine qualities of love, support, compassion and oneness are what the world needs at this time. She comes forth to embrace and unify Her children. Every culture in the world has an expression of Her. Divine Mother is known by many names such as: Lakshmi, Quan Yin, Durga, Kali, Anandamayi Ma, White Buffalo Calf, Mother of Guadalupe and many more. Her deepest desire is to have a personal relationship with each one of us.

My Connection with Divine Mother

In 2014, I followed a dialogue with Divine Mother Class, a wonderful and influential course. She filled me with her unparalleled love, held me, and directed me with Her loving presence. She put me on a bed of roses without thorns, with incommensurable compassion. She healed my wounds and injected me with the divine nectar I needed so badly.

I am forever grateful to Her. It was only when we entered into an intimate relationship that I was able to evoke the power of unconditional love. As the Mother of the universe, she knows exactly what we need and how we feel. She understands our very deep soul's desires. One may sense Her presence in the flowers, in the rain, in the heart. She is everywhere, and Her wisdom and love are infinite. Divine Mother, there are no words to express how much I appreciate Your love and dedication to all of us!

Beloved reader, if you are as I was, perhaps not aware of Her existence, I kindly invite you to reconnect with Her. She is there waiting to be noticed and ready to extend Her hand and lift you from any difficulty you may encounter in life. Just let Her guide you. You will never regret doing it.

Divine Mother Tools

Divine Mother has many tools which we can constantly use. Connie Huebner has created a book wherein all of them are compressed together. By using them, we can transform the energy in, out and around us in an impressive way. They will place you in a place of power. You will feel re-energized and happier just by reading them. Her book is titled *Divine Mother Tools*.

"I am Divine Mother.
I come in the name of peace.
I come in the name of God.
The heart contains all the mysteries of life,
all the mysteries of love.
I am here with you to guide you through this phase of your life,

through the realization of your dreams,
to fill you with love."

Throughout Divine Mother classes, I learned a number of interesting techniques to assist lost souls to go into the light. This has been my greatest tool to deal with psychic attacks, negative entities, or confused souls that don't move forward after departing this planet.

My intention in sharing this topic is to make it more accessible to everybody. One does not need special education or training to help lost souls go into the light. Here are some examples.

A Friend's Parents Went into the Light Many Years after Passing

One day, I was having lunch with a friend in Miami. She mentioned that she was having a recurrent dream about her parents, who had passed many years before. She used to clean her mother's business with great dedication. Her mother, however, never paid her anything for this work. In the dream, her parents were in a dark and dirty place, which surprised her, for her mother used to be extremely clean and organized when she was alive. In the dream, my friend told them that they owed her money, and they denied it and began arguing. Every night it was the same story. My friend looked very confused.

We finished lunch and walked around the mall, but I had this feeling that we needed to spend more time together. I asked her to have some tea at a coffee place. During that time, she mentioned the dream again. I was listening and sensing the energies around us. All of a sudden, I felt the energy of Mother Mary inspiring me to go deep within the situation and, as I focused more on it, I felt the presence of her parents, which made me realize they were not at peace.

I told my friend what I was sensing and asked her: "*What would you tell your mother if you had her in front of you now?*" She insisted that her mother should have paid for her dedication. At the end, she was able to express the best things from her heart and, as soon as she did, her parents were surrounded and taken by a brilliant column of light. It was a beautiful release. My body was trembling, and I had goosebumps all over. They could rest in peace now.

My friend was astounded. She was not totally aware of everything that happened. But, even so, she felt the energy of love and realized that her parents had been suffering because she had hung onto the assumption that they owed her something.

It is my understanding that when we pass on in an unexpected way, leaving unresolved issues or in a very low state of consciousness, it is very easy to get stuck in the astral level, or even to realize that we are dead. Likewise, the fear of judgment or the desire to continue experiencing addictions can prevent us from moving forward.

Healing Many Entities or Lost Souls at Once

One day, I noticed that the cat refused to go outside the cabin. I went out to investigate the reason and sensed a very heavy density. It made me nauseous and then a headache hit me. I realized there were many lost souls and astral entities out there. I knew I had to perform a healing, even though I had never performed a healing on so many entities at one time. I asked Divine Mother for guidance and went back outside. Standing on the deck, I called upon Divine Mother-Father God, Mother Mary, and the Angelic Realm, and addressed the souls in an improvised speech: *"Dear Ones: You deserve to be free. You deserve to be happy. Only by trusting you can achieve these goals. I am going to open a vortex of light for you to go with the angels and Mother Mary. You are blessed, forgiven and released. Come, go with the angels."* After repeating that for a while, I thanked the Divine Beings and went back inside. I was a little afraid at some point but kept trusting that nothing could harm me if I stayed in the light. A few minutes later, the cat and I went outside and noticed that the energy had cleared. Like a miracle, the density had dissipated. I truly believe they listen and, most of the time, are honest and ready to find solace in the light. My intention is that you feel confident and start doing that too.

I used to believe that opening a vortex was a complicated task reserved for experienced people in the field. I have found out that this is an inaccurate notion. Anybody with pure intention and an open heart may do so. The first thing is to ask for divine intervention. You may call for the presence of Mother Mary or the Angels to escort them to the perfect place for them. Afterward, extend your hands to the sky and imagine a door, a vortex of light opening up there. Tell them that they need to be in concordance and freedom, and that the angels are ready to take them. Move your hands like you are pushing something into the vortex. Keep doing it until you feel a relief. In doing so, you assist not just them but also humanity. One act of kindness generates peace on Earth.

Guiding Lost Souls to Find Their Way Home Is a Privilege

Mother Mary came forth with a beautiful message through the powerful Oracle Judith K. Moore, enlightening me about dealing with lost souls on a frequent basis.

> *"It is important for you to know that many unresolved spirits, discordant souls, agents of fear and lost souls are drawn to your light just as a thirsty man is drawn to a holy water, to a spring to partake of the light-giving water."*

This message can be applied to extremely sensitive beings like me, although I must admit that there are times when I may lose my cool and cry out to Mother Mary and Archangel Michael: *"Why has this or that happened?"* I do this especially when I have to clear my space more than once a day, or when they come by the hundreds, or when they just refuse to go in peace. Every day brings a lesson. My daily lesson is to open my heart in compassion to see every challenge as a blessing.

I Have Been a Lost Soul, Too!

During a soul retrieval session, the first thing that appeared before me was a lady, probably in her thirties. She guided me into a beautiful home that was surrounded by luscious green and had a great view of the ocean. It was very well decorated inside. As we entered the house, I noticed that a man, her husband, was organizing documents into a briefcase. However, he did not acknowledge her.

Then I saw her getting into a modern red convertible. I felt the tragedy coming and began crying uncontrollably. I saw the car miss a turn on an ocean curve and somersault over a cliff. I was horrified. It took me a while to continue. At that moment, I realized that the reason the man, her husband, did not acknowledge her was because she was dead and not just that, she was me!

Oh, wow! I was perplexed.

Then I saw the same lady walking barefoot in the woods wearing the same dirty clothing and directing me to a big, abandoned castle-style home. I tried to enter but the doors and windows were sealed. I had a vision in which a lady, who was apparently me, was seated on a chair. A man came with a gun to shoot her in the heart. I felt that she knew the man—a family member, perhaps.

Reflection

Apparently, my own soul came to guide me and show me these two accidental deaths. My soul got stuck and needed my assistance. It sounds like a riddle, but isn't it beautiful the way everything is orchestrated?

Another thing that made me meditate on this type of session was my prior and evident fear of driving on roads similar to the one on which the lady died in the accident. I am convinced that many traumas come from past lives. This type of healing can be complex, but it helps us to move forward in life.

> *"I am Mother-Father God Most High.*
> *I want to give you some teaching about Faith.*
> *Faith is the conviction that everything is given according to a Divine Plan,*
> *and it is what the majority of humans should apply with more frequency*
> *for, without it, things may seem to go in the wrong direction.*
> *Faith must be your inner force,*
> *the force that pushes you to continue, even if you are not getting what*
> *you expected.*
> *Let us use our faith together and nothing will stop you anymore.*
> *There will be no doubts, no fears,*
> *only conviction that all will end up well.*
> *Believe in yourself, believe in your inner power,*
> *in Me within you,*
> *in the force that comes from your heart."*

Maria Magdalene's Message to Humanity through Judith K. Moore

This message has influenced my soul immensely. It came with such an intensity that I felt the need to share it with you. Enjoy it.

"I am the Immortal Magdala. I awaken the Soul of Humanity. I have awakened the visionaries and messengers who carry the energy codes for my immortal consciousness. I have touched each heart with the light of the Beloved and the promise of the awakening of the Divine Feminine within the souls of humanity. The veil is lifting on the face of the Mother God. No longer shall I be denied my place beside my Beloved.

The power of the divine feminine has been waiting for the veil to lift. The seeds for the awakening of the human heart and soul have lain deep within the loam of consciousness. They are the seeds my Beloved spoken about in the parable of the faith of the mustard seed and the seeds that fall on fertile loam.

The seeds have patiently waited for the time when Creation pours forth the living waters to soften the loam of consciousness, awaiting the coming of the conception of the Great Light on Earth. The Divine Feminine God Force is the Womb of Creation, which is the womb of life. I awaited the Union of the Beloved to conceive the Children of the Christ. You are my sons and daughters. You have many names and one heart.

There are numerous mythologies that have been received by my messengers and brought to the world. They all differ in the details of my life, my children, and my roles as a prophetess of light. Yet there is one truth. It is the devotion of Love that spanned the centuries and became a living presence in the world. They encourage you, my Beloveds, to think beyond the limits of fact and to open to mysticism and the mysteries hidden beyond the veil in the non-physical realms.

I touch you and you feel the same power that inspired the Renaissance and religious artists through time to paint me in devotion at the foot of my Beloved. They painted my humble form as I anointed him at the last supper. They depicted me standing beside Mother Mary. And always they portrayed me touching him with my love. I am often seen in their sacred art as wearing a red dress, carrying the alabaster jar, and with a skull at my feet.

Every artist felt me and desired to capture the beauty and mystical power of my living presence because they felt my eternal soul, because I touched them as I touch you now. These are archetypal symbols that endured the oppression of the patriarchal order that denied me, for there is not a human power of will that can ultimately oppress the power of the Divine Feminine I embody, because it is a God Force.

I am the Immortal Magdala, an enigma that defies understanding. I cannot be oppressed because I will rise up amongst you eternally. My power is visible, although my story was not told. Now the stories are spread like seeds of power *through each of my messengers. Each seed is a seed of the Tree of Life, which will blossom and flourish in the Garden of Peace of the New Earth. Do not struggle or even try to know who I AM, for I will elude you. It is only through the power of visionary forces that you may know me by receiving me in your heart. I have many faces and forms. My images are the faces of women throughout time. My eyes are filled with courage and my heart with love; I am you.*

I weep for humanity as I wept for the wounds of humanity that my Beloved embodied. I heal humanity as I healed the wounds of humanity that my Beloved embodied. I witness your resurrection as I was the witness of his resurrection. I am the mighty power of God that restored the wounded Christ in the tomb, and now in the world for the resurrection of the human soul.

I met him in the garden and carried the message to the apostles. 'The tomb of death is empty; he is not there. He lives as I live eternally. You have pushed aside the stone that kept you entombed in the tomb of death to enter the womb of life and be born with the sacred power and knowledge of your divinity living with you.

I witnessed my Beloved's ascension and his return to the living body, for he transcended death and so shall the world. It is only by the power of the miraculous redemption that this shall be, and it is forgiveness. Forgive yourself and forgive others. Forgive those who bear the wounds of the world with their pain. Have faith.

They too shall come to the living waters and heal. They shall know the power of love, and the power of love will heal their wounded souls.

I am not the judge of humanity. I am the Mother of Compassion. I do not stand above you to be worshiped as divine. I am within you. Love yourself and you will know my love, for my love is without limits, it is eternal, and it is a living power of the Mighty Oneness, the Infinite love of Creation.

This message is a message of prophecy. It is given through the power of the Oracle of Creation. It is alchemical. The power of sacred alchemy is contained within the power of the Faith of the mustard seed. It is a force of action spoken of in the words of the Beloved Jesus the Christ. 'If you have the faith of a mustard seed you can move mountains' and 'What I have done, you will do, only greater.'

This is a prophecy, beloved ones, one that is manifest through the heart and soul of humanity of all faiths and beliefs, for there is not a difference between one person's faith and another's when they embrace love. It is all sacred and divine. The mythologies I have sent to the worlds now speak to this. One person will find truth and meaning in one message and not another. The other person will seek and find a truth that has meaning to them in yet another message.

Be that of any religious faith, love is the language of the Infinite Oneness, the Creator of All That Is. As long as the message is of love and inspires faith, it is true for the individual who hears it and sees the power of it working to make their lives whole. The message will bring healing to their hearts and awaken their souls. When it is love without limits, compassion, and faith, it is truth.

That is why God sent so many different messengers to earth. That is why the messengers speak all languages and honor all traditions. They are the messengers of the Way. The diversity of humanity honors the traditions of the ages that are found in the devotion of those who love and are loved.

Yes, my beloved ones, there is not One Story that is true. The Greater Myth unlocks the psyche and opens the awareness to new dimensions of light.

I am the Immortal Magdala, I am the Feminine Christ.

Blessed Be, So Be It, So It Is."

A Vision of The Crucifixion

One evening in May of 2019, I connected with the sacred Maria Magdalene presence and asked if she wanted to include anything in this book. I began speaking a strange tongue as soon as I tried mechanical writing. This is what I wrote:

Great light is pouring into me, and a strong wind is flowing. It is cloudy, and I can feel the density and the sadness around me. I heard: "*I live in your heart.*"

I have been transported to another time. I see a woman's face covered by a mantle. Very windy—it is the time of the crucifixion! I see women crying. I am crying, too!

I heard: "*Open your heart. Allow me to guide you.*" Frightened, I asked: "*Why this space?*" I heard Magdalene's voice: "*There were a few different times, or opportunities, or places.*"

Me: "*I see.*"

My heart felt the most excruciating pain ever. Heartbreaking—how much pain can a human handle?

My head is moving rhythmically back and forth. I see the face of a man—it's Him! Dark hair, dark eyes. I want to listen clearly and do it perfectly.

Maria Magdalene: "*I saw what you did yesterday at the Trail of Tears. I want to tell you that I am very proud of you.*"

Me: "*Thank you.*"

Maria Magdalene: "*Yes, this is Maria Magdalene.*"

Me: "*I am happy you are here.*"

I see the face of Jesus Christ. I see him with a crown of thorns. Now I see a huge stone.

"*I want to see him full of light and power,*" I said out loud. When I did, the vision vanished.

I cannot describe the pain I felt and how alive the scene was! It was so real. I couldn't believe it! It is out of my scope to understand how they could take so much pain. I still cry and shudder. I feel like there is a needle in my heart. It took me a while to recover from it. I am humbled. According to her message above, I would say that she was the one who moved the stone from his tomb and healed his wounds. How? I feel it is beyond human understanding. Thank you, Divine Magdala.

Damage from the Catholic Church Teachings

Being raised as Catholic, I grew up distant from my divine self. Gradually, I began to see the truth and became more dissatisfied with their teachings, dogmas, rituals, lies, and services that are designed to indoctrinate the minds of the credulous. Those lies about a punishing God who instills fear to keep us enslaved are way gone from my psyche. I am now certain that my power resides within. Thanks to Divine Mother's teachings, I connected with the wisdom of my heart. Her teachings empowered me to move forward, even in the worst of the battles.

Mother Mary

The Queen of Heaven

Mother Mary comes at this time to embrace us with Her love, purity and compassion. She wants to be noticed by all Her children on Earth. It may sound strange, but She has always been by you. Give Her all your worries and traumas. She has the ability to transmute them into light and love.

Within the Heart of God, I Am

Excerpt taken from "Mother Mary's Rosary" for an Ascending humanity, received by Patricia Cota-Robles:

> *Hail Mother, full of Grace, the Lord is with Thee.*
> *Blessed are Thou amongst women and blessed is the fruit of thy womb.*
> *"I AM." Hold for us now the immaculate concept of our true God reality from this moment until our Eternal Ascension in the Light.*

I AM THAT I AM.

As a child, I always dreamt of having an encounter with Her. However, with time, her image faded away, compromised by the pressure of daily struggles.

In 2012, I had a session with a great healer who told me that Mother Mary was there and wanted to put a present in my hands. She blessed me for choosing forgiveness over hatred. I was clueless. At that time, I was just starting to ask questions about divinity. Days later, while in meditation, she appeared in my third eye and showed me to place her statue within a bougainvillea plant located in my patio. Excited and grateful, I followed her petition promptly.

When my mother came to visit, she brought a beautiful blue mantle she had created, sewed with golden edges, which we placed upon Her. It rained hard throughout the night, and the following day the mantle and its golden borders were discolored and stained. Although we were sad, and even contemplated the idea of making another mantle, we did not do so.

The following morning, when I went to see Mother Mary, to my surprise the mantle appeared meticulously clean. Although it had rained once again the night before, we knew in our hearts that the sparkling appearance could not have been caused by the rain, because it looked like new! The disappearance of the mantle's discoloration and stains will always remain a mystery, but I know for sure that this was Her intervention.

Another anecdote: One day I received a text message from someone about a very disturbing event she was going through. I was traveling as a passenger in a car and could not do anything to help her. I was about to cry in anguish when suddenly I heard on the radio the Beatles' song *"Let it Be."* And something happened. I clearly understood the lyrics for the first time! I immediately recognized that it was Mother Mary's intercession that worked marvelously, for I got into a very calm state of mind.

Mother Mary has been my refuge in moments of distress, and whenever I ask for Her assistance, She always provides me with a response, through a thought, song, book or animal. I constantly feel her presence guiding and protecting me.

I feel home.
I feel Your Love.
I hear Your voice, and
It is marvelous!
We are connected, Divine Ma.

"I Want the World to See My Tears"

One day while walking past Her altar, I heard the word "*clear.*" The day went by normally; however, the next morning as soon as I opened my eyes, I heard: "*Clear the statue.*" I jumped out of bed, grabbed it, took it to the bathtub, gave it a shower and placed it on top of the sink. Then I began drying her from top to bottom; however, when I looked up at her, I could see a tear in her left eye. I was very surprised, for I had dried her face already. I asked: "*Are you crying? Why are you crying?*" While taking her back to the room, I heard:

> "*Humanity will be crying soon.*
> *Forget about the daily worries of the material world,*
> *and instead, bring your attention within and get to know thyself.*
> *No judgment,*
> *the world is going through turbulent times.*
> *No more disputes,*
> *stay in your heart.*"

Her message came on the full moon of April 29, 2018. I did not sleep that night, nor I could stop crying. Every strong energy lasted for three days in my place. I asked Her if I should share that message with the world, and She replied: "*No, unless you can explain the meaning.*" So, I shared it with just a few persons.

Since I was going through a hard time believing if the message was authentic, I asked my beloved teacher, Connie Huebner, for advice, and Mother Mary came forth with the following:

> "*My message was not meant to frighten you, but to inform you that changes are coming, that many people will be shocked by the changes, and there is a purpose. The human race has not been living in a good way, and I want people to know that they have to change. I want people to know that love is the only way to move forward, but people are resisting love. They are mistrusting each other, they are harming each other, they are hurting each other, and this leads to pain. I don't want the pain to come to my children. I want my children to live joyfully. You are one of my joyful children who has done so much to transmute the energies of pain in the world, and the reason that I communicated this message to you is so you can help me by continuing to do what you have always done, and that is, wherever there is darkness, bringing light, wherever there is fear, bringing love, wherever there is pain, bringing healing.*

I am telling you, as one of my healers, that a change is coming, and it may appear to be negative, but the negative is not going to last. The crying of humanity that I spoke of is a resurrection, a purification, a breakthrough. I want you to know about this so you can stay centered and strong and know that this is a passage through which the human race is passing into a more highly evolved state. I made this statement, no judgment. Don't judge as good or bad. These turbulent times are breaking through to something new. Stay in your heart. Go within. I will take care of you. I love you. There are times in life when there is nothing to do except go deep within, where you are stable, and hold the power there. The power will sustain you and guide you. Be the tower of light, and you will pass through this time and come into the Garden."

Two months later, I had the same feeling to clean her statue. I followed the same procedure, and another tear appeared in her right eye. I said: *"May I take a picture of you this time?"* She agreed. Then, as I asked: *"May I share this picture with others?"* I heard: *"I want the world to see my tears."* And the following message came along:

"I want you to believe in the power of Love.
Love can destroy barriers that only the mind can create.
Connect with the reality of your Heart.
No matter how turbulent the world seems,
Stay in your heart."

This time, I arranged a page with her picture and message and posted it where allowed. Today, I feel her energy telling me that it is time to distribute both messages. I do not know when this book will come out, but I just hope that we have had time to prepare our hearts for what is coming, and to follow her main desire: *"Be a tower of light to guide others."*

God's Calling Us Back Home

Mother Mary inspired me to go deeper into the legendary song *"Stairway to Heaven,"* by Led Zeppelin. One morning, I awoke humming it in my mind. I had probably heard it before but was unaware of the details. I checked it online to find all the specifics. Nothing happened at that time, but a year later it came back, waking me up in the wee hours. This time, I went through the lyrics and ended up listening to the song many times, captivated by its beauty and impeccable composition. After that, the song kept chasing me; it would not go away. I decided to meditate on it and realized that this extraordinary musical work is an insightful message from Mother Mary. Corroboration came as my body got goosebumps while writing this note. My opinion follows.

Stairway to Heaven

The lyrics of the song expose a confrontation between the mundane and spiritual worlds. The symbol of a lady wishing to reach heaven through wealth exposes the heavy density that has surrounded humanity for eons. We all might have fallen for the belief that material things can buy spiritual comfort—this truth came in the form of a metaphor emphasizing the wrong perception that has controlled our world.

The song is a divine message perfectly channeled by the whole group. For those who stay tuned, "the piper" will lead us to reason, a new Earth will dawn, and life will be filled with joy (laughter). I take "the piper" to mean the Creator. It makes sense, doesn't it?

I love when it says: *"If there is a bustle in your hedgerow don't be alarmed now, it's just a spring clean for the May Queen."*

The May Queen? The whole world knows that May is Mother Mary's month. She comes to state the truth behind our free will: There are two paths we can go by, but in the long run, there is still time to change the road you are on—the power of the heart or what the ego mind dictates. The first brings freedom while the latter enslaves—we choose. Nonetheless, there is always an opportunity to change one's path to whatever suits the soul better.

The events coming in the world are mentioned here, as well. It is evident that scandalous things may happen—but don't be afraid, for a cleansing of all that does not serve us will have to go. For those who are not happy with the road they are on, there is still time to change direction. *"The Piper is calling us to join him."* The Piper is a metaphor for God.

God is calling us back home, and that will never stop. A last call: *"Don't you see that your egos' desires lie on the whispering wind?"* Material belongings are weak, for they may vanish in a blink of an eye. Earthquakes, tsunamis, natural disasters, as well as a volatile stock market are examples of that.

As we continue walking on this planet, our shadows are taller than our souls, giving more power to what is seen with our physical eyes than going deep within to see the riches the heart holds. Here is the best part of all: "*There walks a lady we all know, who shines white light and wants to show how everything still turns to gold.*"

Who is that lady we all know, surrounded by a powerful, sparkling white light? She keeps saying that we can turn all into gold once we recognize our own power. Many religions might know her by other names, but She is the representative of the Feminine Force of God. Mother Mary!

Amazingly, it continues: "*If you listen very hard, the tune will come to you at last—when All are One and One Is All.* "

That is the final truth, we are all ONE. When we remember the true essence that we all come from the same Source and humbly see each other as brothers and sisters, we will set ourselves free and can stop the wheel of reincarnation repeating the birth-death cycle we have been attached to for eons.

What an impactful, divine message this song is. No wonder how this song has been played around the world millions of times, its essence touches our hearts in a subtle yet powerful way. I would like to add that I have composed a song which depicts us united as ONE. I hope one day we All sing it together.

Heaven on Earth

And that lady who used to believe that all glitters was gold …
While wanting to buy entrance to heaven
has come to understand that façades can trick us big time … big time.
She wants to share her learning with ALL.

Oh, oh, oh
With ALL …
For she has gotten a present from heaven.
Ooh, oh, from heaven.
Her hands keep shining light to aid others.
Now her biggest dream has become to bring heaven on Earth.
Ooh, oh,
Heaven on Earth.
She has come to believe that thoughts are results of one's faith,
For they shape our fate.

Within the Heart of God, I Am

Love the ego mind for it is not to be resisted ...
Now that the West and the East are dancing together
And the spirit is filled with joy.

Ooh, oh, oh
Overjoyed ... not wondering ...
The moment has come where all are attuned, and the Piper
shall echo with laughter.
Rejoice, laughter that sounds in the forest, for we ALL
are standing together
together at last...

We are ready for changes, not afraid for what's coming,
for we all shall be singing TOGETHER.
Ooh, ooh, no more wondering

The two roads have become just one single road,
A road for heaven.

Join this moment—join this moment ...
Ooh, ooh—ALL together.

Mother Mary, the shining light lady has come to help us remember
that we are ALL ONE AND ONE IS ALL.
The secret to an eternal golden life ...

Ooh, ooh,
No more wonder, all together.
Peace on Earth, peace on Earth as in heaven ...
The veil of illusion has come down and the light's shining upon
Us—together in UNITY, forgiving each other and
welcoming heaven on Earth forever ...
The tune has come to us at last.
WE are ALL ONE and One is All.
Yeah.
We are rocking and not rolling ...
UNITED AS ONE, WE GO ...
Ooh, oh, oh ...
No more wonder... ONLY ONENESS ...

CHAPTER VIII
MY CREATIONS - GOD AND ME

"I love being near nature,
it makes me happy,
instantly connects me with YOU, my Divine Creator.
Because you are the most wonderful expression of happiness.
You are, in fact, the definition of happiness.
You are the definition of joy.
The definition of LOVE.
You are Nature."

I would call my drawings the Epitome of Asymmetry. Symmetry seems to avoid my drawings.

The Story Around Them

In 2014, Ascended Master Vywamus advised me to imprint my feelings on a piece of paper. Years later, in 2019, Mother Mary suggested I include them in this writing. Each one contains a mystical meaning that goes beyond physical observation. Open your heart and meditate on it. Each one has its own connotation. Allow their intrinsic essence to fill your being. They were made out of my great love for you. Their intention is to be used to explore oneself and your place in the universe. Sacred Geometry can be found in nature, in human DNA, in cells, as well as in the architecture of our civilization.

I Am Healthy—I Am Beautiful

This drawing may be used to instill self-love and acceptance of your own body. One may print it and rest the left hand on it while settling down with eyes closed and focusing on the heart area. Repeat positive affirmations about your body. Loving suggestions are: *"I am healthy," "I am beautiful," "I love my body and every part of it," "I respect my body,"* and *"I honor my body."* Smile and envision yourself filled with green light. If you are experiencing any discomfort at the moment, visualize light coming from your heart directly into that area. Smile and trust the process of self-healing. Acceptance of your physical appearance is vital to remain aligned and balanced. You have the power to change any condition in your body. Just believe it.

I Love Myself

Self-love has been encrypted in each dot and point of this lovely graphic. It intends to assist you in achieving more love and acceptance of yourself. When we love ourselves, we are able to love and understand others. It acts as a boomerang. It reverts toward us. Put your attention on it, make a copy, and try to retrace it. Breathe deeply and slowly and think loving thoughts about yourself.

Make a list of the things you have achieved in your life. Little and big things are equally worthy in your heart. Hug and kiss yourself as a gesture of appreciation for all you have done. You are an amazing being of love and light who deserves your own recognition.

To my beloved Sananda, Jesus the Christ,

> *"I love you. Every time I look at your picture,*
> *I feel your presence, your love.*
> *I feel connected to you in a very subtle yet powerful way.*
> *You are my love, the love of my eternal life,*
> *my everything, even though I enjoy serving on Earth*
> *and try to see divinity in each human being,*
> *my biggest joy shall come when we reunite in heaven."*

The Frequency of Gratitude

The heart melts down when the frequency of gratitude touches the soul.

The feeling of gratitude takes us to a place where creation is possible. Make a list of the things that you are grateful for. This will assist you in reaching a higher state of consciousness and, as a result, will attract more of what gives you joy. Take a look at this drawing for a few minutes and then close your eyes, retaining its energy within. Allow the energy to run through your body and mind. It will fill your being with divine rapture.

These are for you.
I am grateful for my perfect body, soul and spirit. (Even if you don't believe your body is perfect, say it! Because it is.)
I am grateful for being on Earth right now.
I am grateful for all that I have—and for all that I don't have.
I am grateful for my life—I am grateful for my death.
I am grateful for all I can see—I am grateful for all I cannot see.
I am grateful for the light—I am grateful for the darkness.
I am grateful for my joy—I am grateful for my sorrows.
I am grateful for my friends—I am grateful for my enemies.
I am grateful for the Sun—I am grateful for the rain.
I am grateful for my smile—I am grateful even if I don't smile.
I am grateful for the trees—I am grateful for the desert.

I am grateful when I can eat—I am grateful when I am fasting. And even if I cannot be grateful, I am grateful!

The Energy Of Devotion

"My wonderful & lovely Nameless One,
I adore you.
Today, I want to tell you how important YOU are in my life,
how beautiful YOU are,
how much I admire YOU.
YOU are my hero of all times,
my GREATEST love.
I love You, God.
I am grateful, I am grateful, I am grateful."

Devotion moves into wisdom.

Devotion is that ardent desire to commit to what brings us a state of elation. It is a surrender of the ego mind and a leap into the unknown. Just trust that what makes our hearts sing is what we need at the moment. Trust yourself and your intuition and move forward fearlessly to reach that which you have been dreaming about. Be devoted to your own wisdom. See through it, ignore the imperfections, and move forward!

This depiction is nothing but imperfect. It is perfection in imperfection. A potent catalyst of divine will.

Inner Peace

Where there is peace, there is love. Hold your attention to the drawing for a while; then close your eyes and allow your heart to talk to you. Stay still and listen to the beating of your heart. Ask questions and be ready to listen to answers that come from your inner self.

A Thought I Wrote on 5/28/17

I am in this place of stillness, emptiness, absence of disturbance, and quietness. A place where even though there is silence and tranquility, I sense myself turning a cube's facets, like I'm hoping to find an answer, without success. Just waiting for something that is waiting for me but eludes me. What is it? There is no color, no emotion. I don't know. I am just waiting, just expecting. Expectation? Yes? No? I don't know. Should I expect a change, a new coming phase on my journey? Where is that so-awaited thing I tried to find in my books? In my computer? In my mind? Is it perhaps in the wisdom of my heart? In this place of wisdom and unconditional love? But toward whom? Me? Am I drained? Am I completed? Am I waiting for something to happen? What is the next step?

I would say that my intuition was guiding me. Indeed, big changes were about to occur in my life, several challenges that served to uncover the truth, and marked a new beginning on my path.

DIVINE MOTHER came forth with this message:

"BE alert in the heart awareness.
It is a conscious alertness that the thinking mind can serve,
not dictate to.
Love is the real dictator.
The real love is an all-benevolent dictator,
open to your ideas, questions, thoughts and actions at all times.
But Infinite Divine Love must be in charge,
not small, need-based love."

I Am Enough

I am enough and I accept that truth. I am strong. I am powerful. I am a being of light capable of enduring any situation and transmuting it into a learning experience to my highest good and that of all others concerned. Let those concepts be immersed in your being. Feel enough. Feel complete and mighty.

Love and Respect for Our Children

I am including this part about our children based on the fact that a common denominator I have found in every person, which causes pain in different forms, is abuse and neglect in intimacy. Every person abused in childhood carries anger, frustration and low self-esteem. We can start by treating our children the best way possible to reduce the incidence. Constantly make them feel loved and supported. Get to know their opinions, dreams, perspectives, feelings and fears; what they would like to change in their lives and surroundings. By doing that, we enrich our relationships and open the doors to healthier communication. That shall provide them with more self-confidence to assist them in making healthy decisions in their lives.

We have been made to believe that worrying is an act of love, but that is not accurate. We are in fact controlled by fear, and that only causes pain. Instead, we can learn to trust our children's divine selves, their divine path, allowing them to enjoy their choices while we, as parents or grandparents, enjoy freedom from fear. Love without fear allows us to grow and evolve. What do you think?

> *I am Mother-Father God.*
> *I have a message for you.*
> *"Don't be afraid, for I Am with you."*
> *Me: "How can I write as beautifully as you do?"*
> *He: "Just let me guide you. I am here to guide you,*
> *Let me hold you; let me pamper you.*
> *You are safe, the world is yours, love it, take care of it,*
> *fill it with love, peace, understanding,*
> *support your brothers and sisters."*
> *Me: "What can I ask you, if every time I think of you*
> *I only think and feel love?"*
> *"Then ask me questions about love!"*
> *Me: "Is the world ready to hear only thoughts of love?"*
> *"The world is and will be ready when you begin talking*
> *about love, so go ahead and start doing that now."*
> *Me: "How can I start doing it? Do I need to travel great distances*
> *to do it?"*
> *"No, you do not need to travel great distances. You can start*
> *by loving yourself.*
> *Once you love yourself, you will be ready to*
> *start loving everything and everybody around you.*
> *Love those who love you,*
> *love those who seem not to love you,*
> *love those who seem angry and disappointed,*

love the flowers, the animals, the water,
love all without restrictions, without limits."

I was pleasantly surprised by the simplicity of His/Her answers. I had always thought that one might need sophisticated, elegant words that just a few could understand. It inspired me to write my soul:

"Dear God/Goddess,
I want to be swirled in your spiral of Light,
In your spiral of Love.
Take control of my life.
Take my hand and guide me.
Show me the way to Infinity."
Me: "Where are you?"
"I am here with you."
Me: "Are you smiling?"
He: "Yes, I am smiling.
Smiling is relaxing."
Me: "I want to be with you forever through eternity.
My heart is open just for You.
Streaming love, love and love.
I only want to talk about love.
I only want to talk about YOU, because YOU are LOVE."

Scientific Proof That God Lives in Our Hearts

The world is evolving at a very fast pace, and so is the conception of God. Scientists at the Institute of Heart Math discovered that the heart has its own intelligence, separate from the brain, and that it can be tapped into for answers about life's most challenging questions. This intelligence is a vortex of Divine Energy that pulses, glows, and spins in a magnificent three-quarter-time rhythm. I find this information amazing. It becomes obvious that when we rest our attention in the heart area, a supremacy seems to be awakened, the supremacy of our inner wisdom. God lives in our hearts as an actual energy field of extraordinary love, wisdom and power for good.

CHAPTER IX
GALACTIC COMMAND-CONFEDERATION

Galactic—Photographs

It was in April 2014 that different shapes of light began to appear in my photographs. Here is one of them.

My curiosity opened up to questions such as: What is that? Why are they appearing in my photographs? Are they humans? Is someone perhaps behind them, attempting to make contact with me? Many questions came into my mind—I was clueless.

During meditation, when I inquired as to the source and meaning of these photographs, I heard "Galactic Confederation," and the following message was relayed to me:

> *"The human race has been tainted. We are here to help humanity. It is our desire to communicate with you, to express our gratitude and love toward all. It is our desire to assist you to step out of your physical reality. We want to be seen by all. We want all to know that we are here to help. We want all to know that there is only love here for all of you. Thank you."*

Later, I received information that the photographs contained codes capable of adjusting our cellular DNA blueprint, and that there were multidimensional beings coming through the symbols in the photographs whose sole purpose was to bring love and peace. The frequencies came from higher dimensions, some in the form of sacred geometry. The codes assist in shifting one's consciousness as well as expanding our Christ consciousness.

Before this event happened, in 2012, during a session with Misa Hopkins, she kindly stated that I came from a faraway galaxy. I found that senseless and discarded it. However, when the lights began to show up in my photographs, I thought she might be right. Keep reading to find out where I came from.

Who Are the Galactics?

The Galactic races are beings of light that inhabit spaces far away from Mother Earth. I can only relate to the multidimensional beings of light that seek to fulfill the divine plan on Earth as it is in heaven. They are much more advanced than us and have been assisting humanity to ascend into a higher dimension for eons. I have not had a conscious, direct contact with them, but I have felt their loving energy. I have been told that, during our existence on Earth, we have incarnated many times in different galaxies/planets across the universe. There are many universes.

The Arcturians

I mention this benevolent group throughout my book. Their essence embodies the purest unconditional love someone can imagine. To know more about them, I invite you to check the website of Dr. Suzanne Lie www.multidimensions.com, as well as Marilyn Raffael's website: www.onenessofall.com.

They are celestial beings from the Arcturus galaxy, which is the brightest star in the Bootes constellation. Their exclusive objective is to bring peace and awareness from a higher dimension. They are our brothers, and they are reliable.

There are many extraterrestrial races who seek to fulfill the plan on Earth as it is in heaven. Besides the Arcturians, there are the Hathors, the Pleiadians, Sirians, Andromedans, Telos, the Lyrans and the Lemurians, to mention just some. I invite you to do your own exploration and notice how you feel when you mention them. If feelings or some affinity come up, you might be from their galaxy.

Another photograph showing galactic presence.

An Unusual Experience—A Mermaid

In 2016, during my first reading with Julien Wells—a powerful multidimensional being who left the planet too young—he told me that I'd had a few past lives as a mermaid in another galaxy made just of water. I thought it was cool but did not give it much thought. However, just recently, following one of Dr. Joe Dispenza's meditations, I saw myself swimming in a deep ocean as a mermaid surrounded by dolphins and whales! It was deeply, deeply impactful. The person I saw was half woman and half fish—what an experience! I did not see her face. I was like a spectator, watching from outside. I felt great joy. I always had this inclination toward dolphins and whales, and now toward mermaids!

It is my understanding that there are thousands of galaxies with different types of lives and environments. In his book, Sanat Kumara explains that his training as a Solar Logos was done in Venus. That confirms the fact that there is life in other galaxies. It is just different than ours.

Alcazar and the Stargate

I would love to share my admiration toward "The Stargate Experience" guided by a being called Alcazar, whose wisdom is channeled by two beautiful and dedicated beings, Prageet Harris and Julieanne Conard. Prageet also channels "The Commander," who speaks in representation of the Galactic Command in a powerful and magnetizing way. The Galactic Command often sends energy transmissions through the Stargate structure to the workshop participants.

Prageet and Julieanne travel around the world to share these experiences, offering meditation workshops to those who are ready and willing to grow spiritually, elevating the human experience. During the meditations, they guide us to navigate into higher dimensions, conveying great harmony that goes beyond the workshop for daily life transformation.

Due to these fabulous teachings, I have reached a deep sense of awareness and knowledge about my galactic inheritance as well as a boundless joy and peace, for which I am deeply grateful.

Thank you, Divine beings, for sharing these possibilities. To experience for yourself, visit: www.thestargateexperienceacademy.com.

Learnings from The Stargate Experience

I am profoundly grateful to Alcazar as a speaker for the Galactic Command for the array of new things I have learned by listening to Prageet and Julieanne. Amazing insights such as the teaching that unicorns, dragons and mermaids have their own worlds. Yes. It is a complex concept for our minds to comprehend, but it makes sense. How did we know about them? I truly believe they are part of our reality.

Also, I would like to emphasize the beauty and power of the meditations relating to the Essence of Life that Julieanne channels along with Ann Sophie. The focus of this Essence is to generate a strong, visceral Essence energy field for yourself - anytime, anywhere. It is more specifically a self-healing tool. Personally, I feel transported into a place of love and calm. Check their website for free meditations and also for an ongoing training program for anyone interested in learning how to emanate the essence of life.

A Photograph of Sedona, Arizona

If you take a close look at the top of the mountain, or even if you can use a magnifying glass, you can notice holograms on top of the mountain. It is like another world beyond the physical.

This town is known for the vortices of light and the presence of many extraterrestrial ships that live up there. Although they are not visible, one can feel the energy. There is a great deal of duality. Beings of light and beings with less light are everywhere. One time, as I opened the front door to get in the house, I distinguished two very thin figures by the bathroom door floating above the floor. They looked similar to those that Neo fights against in the Matrix movie. I was able to send them into the light by clearing my space; however, being under frequent psychic attacks made it almost impossible to stay there. I used to hike a mountain near my home where I always noticed a juniper tree with some sort of a seat shape. While hiking alone one day, I passed it but could not find it again on my way back, even though it was the same trail. The energy was very dense that day; I never went back.

The Hathors

Lately, I have been attracted and connected to The Hathors. These multi-dimensional beings are an intergalactic civilization that come from another universe. They express only unconditional love and are remarkable healers. They heal through music and sounds uttered by themselves. They used to live many centuries ago, during the times of the great Egyptian civilization.

They are our elder brothers and sisters offering their understanding and learning for those who wish to listen. I understand that they came to Earth guided by their deep love toward Gaia and humanity.

Thank you for taking the time to browse these pages. I would like to finalize my writing with the St. Francis of Assisi's Prayer which has touched the hearts of many. I hope you enjoy it.

"Lord,
Make me an instrument of your peace;
Where there is hatred, let me sow love;
Where there is injury, pardon;
Where there is discord, union;
Where there is doubt, faith;
Where there is despair, hope;
Where there is darkness, light;
And where there is sadness, joy.

Oh, Divine Master,
Grant that I may not so much seek to be consoled, as to console; to be understood, as to understand; to be loved, as to love; for it is in giving that we receive, it is in pardoning that we are pardoned, and it is in dying that we are born to eternal life."

Amen

ACKNOWLEDGMENTS

Teachings and meditations that assisted me in my spiritual development:

Connie Huebner at www.divinemotheronline.net

Divine Channeling Sessions with Judith K. Moore

Corinne Feinberg at www.pathlighthealing.com

Soul Retrieval Sessions with Marcia McMahon at www.enlightenedhypnosis.net

Dr. Joe Dispenza Meditations, workshops and books

Carla Fox at www.quantumstargate.com

Incredible sessions with The Arcturians through Dr. Suzanne Lie at www.suzanneliephd.blogspot.com

The8thfire.com- Shamanism Classes taught by Pete Bernard

Judi Satori—Meditations

Solara An-Ra Meditations

Mas Sajadi Detox Programs

The Stargate Experience- Alcazar's wisdom channeled by Prageet Harris and Julianne Conard.

Commander's wisdom channeled by Prageet Harris.

RELEVANT BOOKS

Dear and Glorious Physician/Saint Luke, by Taylor Caldwell

Messages from the Masters, by Dr. Brian Weiss

The Arcturian Anthology, by Tom Kenyon and Judi Sion

The Keys of Enoch, by J. J. Hurtak

The Magdalene Manuscript, by Tom Kenyon and Judi Sion

Forbidden Knowledge, by Jason Quitt & Bob Mitchell

Earth Expressions: An Artistic Exploration Inspired by Crop Circles, by Catherine Cogorno

Miracle Prayer, by Dr. Susan Shumsky

Radical Forgiveness, by Colin Tipping

The Light Shall Set You Free, by Dr. Norma Milanovich

Conversations with God, by Neale D. Walsch

Crop Circles Revealed, Judith K. Moore

Sanat Kumara—Training a Planetary Logos, Channeled and Edited by Janet McClure

Becoming Supernatural —How Common People Are Doing the Uncommon written by Dr. Joe Dispenza.

I highly recommend Dr. Joe Dispenza's meditations, workshops and books. He is doing a great job teaching us how to get a more healed world. Visit his website at: www.drjoedispenza.com.

Discovering Angels, How to Invite Angels into your Life for Peace, Tranquility, and Personal Change, by Pamela Landolt Green.

About the Author

Lucero Tello, is both subject and object in the book. She is living proof of God's presence in our lives. She recently moved to Washington, DC, to continue her sacred journey.

CPSIA information can be obtained
at www.ICGtesting.com
Printed in the USA
LVHW070839230220
647904LV00027B/2982